T0151012

Birds *of* Arizona

Field Guide

Stan Tekiela

Adventure Publications
Cambridge, Minnesota

Edited by Sandy Livoti and Dan Downing

Cover, book design and illustrations by Jonathan Norberg

Range maps produced by Anthony Hertzel

Cover photo: Vermilion Flycatcher by Stan Tekiela
All photos by Stan Tekiela except pp. 168, 372 (male) by **Agami Photo Agency/Shutterstock.com**; p. 364 (non-breeding male) by **Paul Bannick**; p. 238 (juvenile) by **Albert Barr/Shutterstock.com**; pp. 28, 146 (male) **Gualberto Becerra/Shutterstock.com**; pp. 86 (female), 120 (female), 154 (female), 154 (male), 324, 332 (both), 334 (both), 352 (female), 368 (both) by **Rick & Nora Bowers**; p. 166 by **Gerald A. DeBoer/Shutterstock.com**; p. 212 (soaring) by **Dudley Edmondson**; p. 228 (female) by **Kevin T. Karlson**; pp. 90 (female), 138 (female) by **Brian E Kushner/Shutterstock.com**; p. 364 (female) by **M. Leonard Photography/Shutterstock.com**; p. 258 by **Laura Mountainspring/Shutterstock.com**; p. 318 (female) by **Thomas Morris/Shutterstock.com**; p. 56 by **A. G. Nelson/Dembinsky Photo Associates**; p. 164 by **G. Parekh/Shutterstock.com**; p. 252 by **Scenic Corner/Shutterstock.com**; p. 372 (female) by **Brian E. Small**; pp. 28, 146 (female) by **Stubblefield Photography/Shutterstock.com**; p. 94 (female) by **Sundry Photography/Shutterstock.com**; p. 280 (displaying) by **Hartmut Walter**; pp. 52 (juvenile), 172 (in-flight juvenile & juvenile), 208 (dark morph, intermediate morph & soaring dark morph), 214 (juvenile), 220 (juvenile), 298 (juvenile), 300 (in-flight juvenile) by **Brian K. Wheeler**; and pp. 96, 116 (Oregon female), 206 (female), 272 (inset), 296, 302 (female), 358 (female) by **Jim Zipp**.

To the best of the publisher's knowledge, all photos were of live birds. Some were photographed in a controlled condition.

10 9 8 7 6 5 4

Birds of Arizona Field Guide
First Edition 2003
Second Edition 2021
Copyright © 2003 and 2021 by Stan Tekiela
Published by Adventure Publications
An imprint of AdventureKEEN
310 Garfield Street South
Cambridge, Minnesota 55008
(800) 678-7006
www.adventurepublications.net
All rights reserved
Printed in China
ISBN 978-1-64755-194-0 (pbk.); ISBN 978-1-64755-195-7 (ebook)

TABLE OF CONTENTS

WHAT'S NEW?

It is hard to believe that it's been more than 15 years since the debut of *Birds of Arizona Field Guide*. This critically acclaimed field guide has helped countless people identify and enjoy the birds that we love. Now, in this expanded second edition, *Birds of Arizona Field Guide* has many new and exciting changes and a fresh look, while retaining the same familiar, easy-to-use format.

To help you identify even more birds in Arizona, I have added 8 new species and more than 150 new color photographs. All of the range maps have been meticulously reviewed, and many updates have been made to reflect the ever-changing movements of the birds.

Everyone's favorite section, "Stan's Notes," has been expanded to include even more natural history information. "Compare" sections have been updated to help ensure that you correctly identify your bird, and additional feeder information has been added to help with bird feeding. I hope you will enjoy this great new edition as you continue to learn about and appreciate our Arizona birds!

WHY WATCH BIRDS IN ARIZONA?

Millions of people have discovered bird feeding. It's a simple and enjoyable way to bring the beauty of birds closer to your home. Watching birds at your feeder often leads to a lifetime pursuit of bird identification. The *Birds of Arizona Field Guide* is for those who want to identify common birds of Arizona.

There are over 1,100 species of birds found in North America. In Arizona alone there have been more than 350 different kinds of birds recorded through the years. These bird sightings were diligently recorded by hundreds of bird watchers and became part of the official state record. From these valuable records, I've chosen 153 of the most common birds of Arizona to include in this field guide.

Bird watching, or birding, is one of the most popular activities in America. Its outstanding appeal in Arizona is due, in part, to an unusually rich and abundant birdlife. Why are there so many birds? One reason is open space. Arizona is nearly 114,000 square miles (295,300 sq. km). Despite its size, only about 7 million people call Arizona home. On average, that is only 50 people per square mile (19 per sq. km). Most of these people are located in and around only two major cities located in southern Arizona.

Open space is not the only reason there is such an abundance of birds. It's also the diversity of habitat. Arizona can be broken into three distinct habitats—Colorado Plateau, Transition Zone and the Basin and Range Region—each of which supports different groups of birds.

The Colorado Plateau is located in the northern part of Arizona. It is a relatively flat, dry, semi-desert region with many rivers that have cut deep canyons. Elevation from the bottom of a canyon to its upper rim can change by as much as 5,000 feet (1,500 m). While the Grand Canyon is the most famous, equally impressive are the Oak Creek Canyon and Canyon de Chelly, among others. The Colorado Plateau is the least inhabited part of the state, but it is one of the most beautiful. Ferruginous Hawks, Steller's Jays and many other birds live in this region.

The Transition Zone, formerly known as the Central Highlands, divides Arizona horizontally. Many mountain ranges here are in close proximity and appear as clusters of peaks interspersed with steep-walled valleys. This part of the state is a good place to see Vermilion Flycatchers and Pine Siskins.

South of the Transition Zone is the Basin and Range Region. This region covers most of southern Arizona and is known by most as the Sonoran Desert. The habitat is mainly flat desert separated by mountain ranges. It is a sparsely vegetated area that is home to many wonderful birds such as Black-throated Sparrows and various hummingbird species.

Water also plays a large part in Arizona's bird populations. There are more than 360 square miles (935 sq. km) of water surface in the state. From the Colorado River to the Gila and Salt Rivers, and from Lake Mead, the state's largest reservoir, to Lake Powell and Roosevelt Lake, this essential element supports a variety of water-loving birds such as Red-winged Blackbirds and American Avocets. It's always worth time to investigate any body of water in Arizona for the presence of birds.

Varying habitats in Arizona also mean variations in the weather. Since elevation rises from approximately 140 feet (40 m) to over 10,000 feet (3,050 m) at mountaintops, there are big differences in the weather from northern Arizona to the southern desert. Tall peaks, such as Mount Graham, are some of the coldest, snowiest places in Arizona, while the desert in the southeastern corner of the state remains relatively warm and dry most of the year.

No matter if you are in the hot, dry desert or in the cool, moist mountains of Arizona, there are birds to watch in each season. Whether witnessing hawks migrating in autumn or welcoming back hummingbirds in spring, there is variety and excitement in birding as each season turns to the next.

OBSERVE WITH A STRATEGY: TIPS FOR IDENTIFYING BIRDS

Identifying birds isn't as difficult as you might think. By simply following a few basic strategies, you can increase your chances of successfully identifying most birds that you see. One of the first and easiest things to do when you see a new bird is to note **its color.** This field guide is organized by color, so simply turn to the right color section to find it.

Next, note the **size of the bird.** A strategy to quickly estimate size is to compare different birds. Pick a small, a medium and a large bird. Select an American Robin as the medium bird. Measured from bill tip to tail tip, a robin is 10 inches (25 cm). Now select two other birds, one smaller and one larger. Good choices are a House Sparrow, at about 6 inches (15 cm), and an American Crow, around 18 inches (45 cm). When you see a species you don't know, you can now quickly ask yourself, "Is it larger than a sparrow but smaller than a robin?" When you look in your field guide to identify your bird, you would check the species that are roughly 6–10 inches (15–25 cm). This will help to narrow your choices.

Next, note the **size, shape and color of the bill.** Is it long or short, thick or thin, pointed or blunt, curved or straight? Seed-eating birds, such as Evening Grosbeaks, have bills that are thick and strong enough to crack even the toughest seeds. Birds that sip nectar, such as Black-chinned Hummingbirds, need long, thin bills to reach deep into flowers. Hawks and owls tear their prey with very sharp, curving bills. Sometimes, just noting the bill shape can help you decide whether the bird is a woodpecker, finch, grosbeak, blackbird or bird of prey.

Next, take a look around and note the **habitat** in which you see the bird. Is it wading in a saltwater marsh? Walking along a riverbank or on the beach? Soaring in the sky? Is it perched high in the trees or hopping along the forest floor? Because of diet and habitat preferences, you'll often see robins hopping on the ground but not usually eating seeds at a feeder. Or you'll see a Black-headed Grosbeak sitting on a tree branch but not climbing headfirst down the trunk, like a Red-breasted Nuthatch would.

Noticing **what the bird is eating** will give you another clue to help you identify the species. Feeding is a big part of any bird's life. Fully one-third of all bird activity revolves around searching for food, catching prey and eating. While birds don't always follow all the rules of their diet, you can make some general assumptions. Northern Flickers, for instance, feed on ants and other insects, so you wouldn't expect to see them visiting a seed feeder. Other birds, such as Barn and Cliff Swallows, eat flying insects and spend hours swooping and diving to catch a meal.

Sometimes you can identify a bird by **the way it perches.** Body posture can help you differentiate between an American Crow and a Red-tailed Hawk, for example. Crows lean forward over their feet on a branch, while hawks perch in a vertical position. Consider posture the next time you see an unidentified large bird in a tree.

Birds in flight are harder to identify, but noting the **wing size and shape** will help. Wing size is in direct proportion to body size, weight and type of flight. Wing shape determines whether the bird flies fast and with precision, or slowly and less precisely. Barn Swallows, for instance, have short, pointed wings that slice through the air, enabling swift, accurate flight. Turkey Vultures have long, broad wings for soaring on warm updrafts. House Finches have short, rounded wings, helping them to flit through thick tangles of branches.

Some bird species have a unique **pattern of flight** that can help in identification. American Goldfinches fly in a distinctive undulating pattern that makes it look like they're riding a roller coaster.

While it's not easy to make all of these observations in the short time you often have to watch a "mystery" bird, practicing these identification methods will greatly expand your birding skills. To further improve your skills, seek the guidance of a more experienced birder who can answer your questions on the spot.

BIRD BASICS

It's easier to identify birds and communicate about them if you know the names of the different parts of a bird. For instance, it's more effective to use the word "crest" to indicate the set of extra-long feathers on top of the head of a Steller's Jay than to try to describe it.

The following illustration points out the basic parts of a bird. Because it is a composite of many birds, it shouldn't be confused with any actual bird.

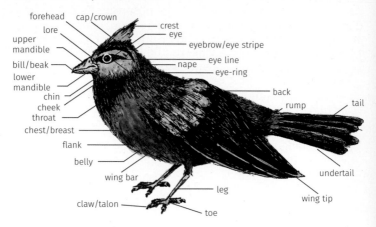

Bird Color Variables

No other animal has a color palette like a bird's. Brilliant blues, lemon yellows, showy reds and iridescent greens are common in the bird world. In general, male birds are more colorful than their female counterparts. This helps males attract a mate, essentially saying, "Hey, look at me!" Color calls attention to a male's health as well. The better the condition of his feathers, the better his food source, territory and potential for mating.

Male and female birds that don't look like each other are called sexually dimorphic, meaning "two forms." Dimorphic females often have a nondescript dull color, as seen in Lazuli Buntings. Muted tones help females hide during the weeks of motionless incubation and draw less attention to them when they're out feeding or taking a break from the rigors of raising the young.

The males of some species, such as the Hairy Woodpecker, Steller's Jay and Bald Eagle, look nearly identical to the females. In woodpeckers, the sexes are differentiated by only a red mark, or sometimes a yellow mark. Depending on the species, the mark may be on top of the head, on the face or nape of neck, or just behind the bill.

During the first year, juvenile birds often look like their mothers. Since brightly colored feathers are used mainly for attracting a mate, young non-breeding males don't have a need for colorful plumage. It's not until the first spring molt (or several years later, depending on the species) that young males obtain their breeding colors.

Both breeding and winter plumages are the result of molting. Molting is the process of dropping old, worn feathers and replacing them with new ones. All birds molt, typically twice a year, with the spring molt usually occurring in late winter. At this time, most birds produce their brighter breeding plumage, which lasts throughout the summer.

Winter plumage is the result of the late summer molt, which serves a couple of important functions. First, it adds feathers for warmth in the coming winter season. Second, in some species it produces feathers that tend to be drab in color, which helps to camouflage the birds and hide them from predators. The winter plumage of the male American Goldfinch, for example, is olive-brown, unlike its canary-yellow breeding color during summer. Luckily for us, some birds, such as the male Lewis's Woodpeckers, retain their bright summer colors all year long.

Bird Nests

Bird nests are a true feat of engineering. Imagine constructing a home that's strong enough to weather storms, large enough to hold your entire family, insulated enough to shelter them from cold and heat, and waterproof enough to keep out rain. Think about building it without blueprints or directions and using mainly your feet. Birds do this!

Before building, birds must select an appropriate site. In some species, such as the House Wren, the male picks out several potential sites and assembles small twigs in each. The "extra" nests, called dummy nests, discourage other birds from using any nearby cavities for their nests. The male takes the female around and shows her the choices. After choosing her favorite, she finishes the construction.

In other species, such as the Bullock's Oriole, the female selects the site and builds the nest, while the male offers an occasional suggestion. Each bird species has its own nest-building routine that is strictly followed.

As you can see in these illustrations, birds build a wide variety of nest types.

| ground nest | platform nest | cup nest | pendulous nest | cavity nest |

Nesting material often consists of natural items found in the immediate area. Most nests consist of plant fibers (such as bark from grapevines), sticks, mud, dried grass, feathers, fur, or soft, fuzzy tufts from thistle. Some birds, including Broad-tailed Hummingbirds, use spiderwebs to glue nest materials together.

Transportation of nesting material is limited to the amount a bird can hold or carry. Birds must make many trips afield to gather enough material to complete a nest. Most nests take four days or more, and hundreds, if not thousands, of trips to build.

A **ground nest** can be a mound of vegetation on the ground or in the water. It can also be just a simple, shallow depression scraped out in earth, stones or sand. Killdeer and Horned Larks scrape out ground nests without adding any nesting material.

The **platform nest** represents a much more complex type of construction. Typically built with twigs or sticks and branches, this nest forms a platform and has a depression in the center to nestle the eggs. Platform nests can be in trees; on balconies, cliffs, bridges, or man-made platforms; and even in flowerpots. They often provide space for the adventurous young and function as a landing platform for the parents.

Mourning Doves and herons don't anchor their platform nests to trees, so these can tumble from branches during high winds and storms. Hawks, eagles, ospreys and other birds construct sturdier platform nests with large sticks and branches.

Other platform nests are constructed on the ground with mud, grass and other vegetation from the area. Many waterfowl build platform nests on the ground near or in water. A **floating platform nest** moves with the water level, preventing the nest, eggs and birds from being flooded.

Three-quarters of all songbirds construct a **cup nest,** which is a modified platform nest. The supporting platform is built first and attached firmly to a tree, shrub, or rock ledge or the ground. Next, the sides are constructed with grass, small twigs, bark or leaves, which are woven together and often glued with mud for added strength. The inner cup can be lined with down feathers, animal fur or hair, or soft plant materials and is contoured last.

The **pendulous nest** is an unusual nest that looks like a sock hanging from a branch. Attached to the end of small branches of trees, this unique nest is inaccessible to most predators and often waves wildly in a breeze.

Woven tightly with plant fibers, the pendulous nest is strong and watertight and takes up to a week to build. A small opening at the top or on the side allows parents access to the grass-lined interior. More commonly used by tropical birds, this complex nest has also been mastered by orioles and kinglets. It must be one heck of a ride to be inside one of these nests during a windy spring thunderstorm!

The **cavity nest** is used by many species of birds, most notably woodpeckers and Western Bluebirds. A cavity nest is often excavated from a branch or tree trunk and offers shelter from storms, sun, cold and predators. A small entrance hole in a tree can lead to a nest chamber that is up to a safe 10 inches (25 cm) deep.

Typically made by woodpeckers, cavity nests are usually used only once by the builder. Nest cavities can be used for many subsequent years by birds such as bluebirds, which do not have the capability to excavate their own. Kingfishers, on the other hand, can dig a tunnel up to 4 feet (about 1 m) long in a riverbank. The nest chamber at the end of the tunnel is already well insulated, so it's usually only sparsely lined.

One of the most clever of all nests is the **no nest,** or daycare nest. Parasitic birds, such as cowbirds, don't build their own nests. Instead, the egg-laden female searches out the nest of another bird and sneaks in to lay an egg while the host mother isn't looking.

A mother cowbird wastes no energy building a nest only to have it raided by a predator. Laying her eggs in the nests of other birds transfers the responsibility of raising her young to the host. When she lays her eggs in several nests, the chances increase that at least one of her babies will live to maturity.

Who Builds the Nest?

Generally, the female bird constructs the nest. She gathers the materials and does the building, with an occasional visit from her mate to check on progress. In some species, both parents contribute equally to nest building. The male may forage for sticks, grass or mud, but it is the female that often fashions the nest. Only rarely does a male build a nest by himself.

Fledging

Fledging is the time between hatching and flight, or leaving the nest. Some species of birds are **precocial,** meaning they leave the nest within hours of hatching, though it may be weeks before they can fly. This is common in waterfowl and shorebirds.

Baby birds that hatch naked and blind need to stay in the nest for a few weeks (these birds are **altricial**). Baby birds that are still in the nest are **nestlings.** Until birds start to fly, they are called **fledglings.**

Why Birds Migrate

Why do so many species of birds migrate? The short answer is simple: food. Birds migrate to locations with abundant food, as it is easier to breed where there is food than where food is scarce. Western Tanagers, for instance, are **complete migrators** that fly from the tropics of Central America and Mexico to nest in the forests of North America, where billions of newly hatched insects are available to feed to their young.

Other migrators, such as some birds of prey, migrate back to northern regions in spring. In these locations, they hunt mice, voles and other small rodents that are beginning to breed.

Complete migrators have a set time and pattern of migration. Every year at nearly the same time, they head to a specific wintering ground. Complete migrators may travel great distances, sometimes 15,000 miles (24,100 km) or more in one year.

Complete migration doesn't necessarily imply flying from the cold, frozen northland to a tropical destination. The Swainson's Hawk, for example, is a complete migrator that flies from Arizona to Central and South America. This trip is still considered complete migration.

Complete migrators have many interesting aspects. In spring, males often leave a few weeks before the females, arriving early to scope out possibilities for nesting sites and food sources, and to begin to defend territories. The females arrive several weeks later. In many species, the females and their young leave earlier in the fall, often up to four weeks before the adult males.

Other species, such as the American Goldfinch, are **partial migrators**. These birds usually wait until their food supplies dwindle before flying south. Unlike complete migrators, partial migrators move only far enough south, or sometimes east and west, to find abundant food. In some years it might be only a few hundred miles, while in other years it can be as much as a thousand. This kind of migration, dependent on weather and the availability of food, is sometimes called seasonal movement.

Unlike the predictable complete migrators or partial migrators, **irruptive migrators** can move every third to fifth year or, in some cases, in consecutive years. These migrations are triggered when times are tough and food is scarce. Red-breasted Nuthatches are irruptive migrators. They leave their normal northern range in search of more food or in response to overpopulation.

Many other birds don't migrate at all. Mountain Chickadees, for example, are **non-migrators** that remain in their habitat all year long and just move around as necessary to find food.

How Do Birds Migrate?

One of the many secrets of migration is fat. While most people are fighting the ongoing battle of the bulge, birds intentionally gorge themselves to gain as much fat as possible without losing the ability to fly. Fat provides the greatest amount of energy per unit of weight. In the same way that your car needs gas, birds are propelled by fat and stall without it.

During long migratory flights, fat deposits are used up quickly, and birds need to stop to refuel. This is when backyard bird feeding stations and undeveloped, natural spaces around our towns and cities are especially important. Some birds require up to 2–3 days of constant feeding to build their fat reserves before continuing their seasonal trip.

Many birds, such as most eagles, hawks, ospreys, falcons and vultures, migrate during the day. Larger birds can hold more body fat, go longer without eating and take longer to migrate. These birds glide along on rising columns of warm air, called thermals, that hold them aloft while they slowly make their way north or south. They generally rest at night and hunt early in the morning before the sun has a chance to warm the land and create good soaring conditions. Daytime migrators use a combination of landforms, rivers, and the rising and setting sun to guide them in the right direction.

The majority of small birds, called **passerines,** migrate at night. Studies show that some use the stars to navigate. Others use the setting sun, and still others, such as pigeons, use Earth's magnetic field to guide them north or south.

While flying at night may not seem like a good idea, it's actually safer. First, there are fewer avian predators hunting for birds at night. Second, night travel allows time during the day to find food in unfamiliar surroundings. Third, wind patterns at night tend to be flat, or laminar. Flat winds don't have the turbulence of daytime winds and can help push the smaller birds along.

HOW TO USE THIS GUIDE

To help you quickly and easily identify birds, this field guide is organized by color. Refer to the color key on the first page, note the color of the bird, and turn to that section. For example, the Red-naped Sapsucker is black and white with red on its head. Because the bird is mostly black-and-white, it will be found in the black-and-white section.

Each color section is also arranged by size, generally with the smaller birds first. Sections may also incorporate the average size in a range, which in some cases reflects size differences between male and female birds. Flip through the pages in the color section to find the bird. If you already know the name of the bird, check the index for the page number.

In some species, the male and female are very different in color. In others, the breeding and winter plumage colors differ. These species will have an inset photograph with a page reference and will be found in two color sections.

You will find a variety of information in the bird description sections. To learn more, turn to the sample on pp. 22–23.

Range Maps

Range maps are included for each bird. Colored areas indicate where the bird is frequently found. The colors represent the presence of a species during a specific season, not the density, or amount, of birds in the area. Green is used for summer, blue for winter, red for year-round and yellow for migration.

While every effort has been made to depict accurate ranges, these are constantly in flux due to a variety of factors. Changing weather, habitat, species abundance and availability of vital resources, such as food and water, can affect the migration and movement of local populations, causing birds to be found in areas that are atypical for the species. So please use the maps as intended—as general guides only.

female
p. 119

male

Common Name

Range Map *Scientific name* Color Indicator

YEAR-ROUND
SUMMER
MIGRATION
WINTER

Size: measurement is from head to tip of tail; wingspan may be listed as well

Male: brief description of the male bird; may include breeding, winter or other plumages

Female: brief description of the female bird, which is sometimes different from the male

Juvenile: brief description of the juvenile bird, which often looks like the adult female

Nest: kind of nest the bird builds to raise its young; who builds it; number of broods per year

Eggs: number of eggs you might expect to see in a nest; color and marking

Incubation: average days the parents spend incubating the eggs; who does the incubation

Fledging: average days the young spend in the nest after hatching but before they leave the nest; who does the most "childcare" and feeding

Migration: type of migrator: complete (seasonal, consistent), partial (seasonal, destination varies), irruptive (unpredictable, depends on the food supply) or non-migrator

Food: what the bird eats most of the time (e.g., seeds, insects, fruit, nectar, small mammals, fish) and whether it typically comes to a bird feeder

Compare: notes about other birds that look similar and the pages on which they can be found; may include extra information to aid in identification

Stan's Notes: Interesting natural history information. This could be something to look or listen for or something to help positively identify the bird. Also includes remarkable features.

female
p. 145

male

Brown-headed Cowbird
Molothrus ater

YEAR-ROUND
SUMMER
WINTER

Size: 7½" (19 cm)

Male: Glossy black with a chocolate-brown head. Dark eyes. Pointed, sharp gray bill.

Female: dull brown with a pointed, sharp, gray bill

Juvenile: similar to female but with dull-gray plumage and a streaked chest

Nest: no nest; lays eggs in nests of other birds

Eggs: 5–7; white with brown markings

Incubation: 10–13 days; host birds incubate eggs

Fledging: 10–11 days; host birds feed the young

Migration: partial to non-migrator in Arizona

Food: insects, seeds; will come to seed feeders

Compare: Male Bronzed Cowbird (p. 29) is slightly larger and has bright-red eyes. The male Red-winged Blackbird (p. 35) is slightly larger with red-and-yellow patches on upper wings. European Starling (p. 27) has a shorter tail.

Stan's Notes: Cowbirds are members of the blackbird family. Of approximately 750 species of parasitic birds worldwide, this is one of two parasitic birds on the state. Brood parasites lay their eggs in the nests of other birds, leaving the host birds to raise their young. Cowbirds are known to have laid their eggs in the nests of over 200 species of birds. While some birds reject cowbird eggs, most incubate them and raise the young, even to the exclusion of their own. Look for warblers and other birds feeding young birds twice their own size. Named "Cowbird" for its habit of following bison and cattle herds to feed on insects flushed up by the animals.

winter

breeding

European Starling
Sturnus vulgaris

YEAR-ROUND

Size:	7½" (19 cm)
Male:	Glittering, iridescent purplish black in spring and summer; duller and speckled with white in fall and winter. Long, pointed, yellow bill in spring; gray in fall. Pointed wings. Short tail.
Female:	same as male
Juvenile:	similar to adults, with grayish-brown plumage and a streaked chest
Nest:	cavity; male and female line cavity; 2 broods per year
Eggs:	4–6; bluish with brown markings
Incubation:	12–14 days; female and male incubate
Fledging:	18–20 days; female and male feed the young
Migration:	non-migrator
Food:	insects, seeds, fruit; visits seed or suet feeders
Compare:	The male Brown-headed Cowbird (p. 25) has a brown head. Look for the shiny, dark feathers to help identify the European Starling.

Stan's Notes: A great songster, this bird can also mimic the songs of up to 20 bird species and imitates sounds, including the human voice. Jaws are more powerful when opening than when closing, enabling the bird to pry open crevices to find insects. Often displaces woodpeckers, chickadees and other cavity-nesting birds. Large families gather with blackbirds in the fall. Not a native bird; 100 starlings were introduced to New York City in 1890–91 from Europe. Bill changes color in spring and fall.

female
p. 147

juvenile

YEAR-ROUND
SUMMER
MIGRATION

Bronzed Cowbird
Molothrus aeneus

Size: 8" (20 cm)

Male: Black plumage with glossy blue wings and tail. A thick, pointed, slightly down-curved black bill. Bright-red eyes. Short tail.

Female: overall dull brown-to-gray bird with darker brown wings and tail, a thick, pointed and slightly downward-curving gray bill, bright-red eyes, short tail

Juvenile: similar to female, but dull-red eyes and bill is lighter in color

Nest: no nest; lays eggs in nests of other birds

Eggs: 5–7; pale bluish green without markings

Incubation: 10–12 days; host bird incubates eggs

Fledging: 10-11 days; host birds feed young

Migration: complete migrator, to Mexico; some stay year-round in a small part of Arizona

Food: insects, seeds; comes to ground feeders

Compare: Similar to the male Brown-headed Cowbird (p. 25), which has a brown head and lacks the Bronzed Cowbird's bright-red eyes.

Stan's Notes: One of two parasitic bird species in Arizona. Adults are easy to identify and differentiate from other birds by their bright red eyes. During courtship, male throws head back, ruffles feathers and bounces up and down in front of female. Usually seen in small flocks with other species. Most are migrators, but some remain in southwestern Arizona. Known to parasitize over 70 species of birds. Female pierces host bird's eggs, which kills the young, then lays her eggs in the nest. Some birds reject cowbird eggs, but most incubate them and raise the young, even to the exclusion of their own.

female
p. 267

male

Phainopepla
Phainopepla nitens

Size: 8" (20 cm)

Male: Slim, long, glossy black bird with a ragged crest and deep red eyes. Wing patches near tips of wings are white, obvious in flight.

Female: slim, long, mostly gray bird with a ragged crest and deep red eyes, whitish wing bars

Juvenile: similar to female

Nest: cup; female and male construct; 1–2 broods per year

Eggs: 2–4; gray with brown markings

Incubation: 12–14 days; female and male incubate

Fledging: 18–20 days; female and male feed young

Migration: complete, to southern Arizona and California

Food: fruit (usually mistletoe), insects; will come to water elements or water drips in yards

Compare: The only all-black bird with a crest and red eyes. Look for white wing patches in flight.

Stan's Notes: Seen in desert scrub with water and mistletoe nearby. Gives a low, liquid "kweer" song, but will also mimic other species. In winter, individuals defend food supply, such as a single tree with abundant mistletoe berries. Probably responsible for the dispersal of mistletoe plants far and wide. Male will fly up to a height of 300 feet (90 m), circling and zigzagging to court female. Builds nest of twigs and plant fibers and binds it with spider webs in the crotch of a mistletoe cluster. Lines nest with hair or soft plant fibers. May be the only species to nest in two regions in the same nesting season. Nests in dry desert habitat in early spring, and when it gets hot, moves to a higher area with an abundant water supply to nest again.

Spotted Towhee

Pipilo maculatus

Size: 8½" (22 cm)

Male: Mostly black with dirty red-brown sides and a white belly. Multiple white spots on wings and sides. Long black tail with a white tip. Rich, red eyes.

Female: very similar to male but with a brown head

Juvenile: brown with a heavily streaked chest

Nest: cup; female builds; 1–2 broods per year

Eggs: 3–5; white with brown markings

Incubation: 12–14 days; female and male incubate

Fledging: 10–12 days; female and male feed young

Migration: non-migrator to partial migrator; moves around in winter to find food

Food: seeds, fruit, insects

Compare: Closely related to the Green-tailed Towhee (p. 323), which lacks the bold black and red colors. American Robin (p. 279) is larger.

Stan's Notes: Not as common as the Green-tailed Towhee, but it inhabits similar habitat. Found in a variety of habitats, from thick brush and chaparral to suburban backyards. Usually heard noisily scratching through dead leaves on the ground for food. Over 70 percent of its diet is plant material. Eats more insects during spring and summer. Well known to retreat from danger by walking away rather than taking to flight. Nest is nearly always on the ground under bushes but away from where the male perches to sing. Begins breeding in April. Lays eggs in May. After the breeding season, moves to higher elevations. Song and plumage vary geographically and aren't well studied or understood.

female
p. 161

male

YEAR-ROUND

Red-winged Blackbird
Agelaius phoeniceus

Size: 8½" (22 cm)

Male: Jet black with red-and-yellow patches (epaulets) on upper wings. Pointed black bill.

Female: heavily streaked brown with a pointed brown bill and white eyebrows

Juvenile: same as female

Nest: cup; female builds; 2–3 broods per year

Eggs: 3–4; bluish green with brown markings

Incubation: 10–12 days; female incubates

Fledging: 11–14 days; female and male feed the young

Migration: non-migrator; will move around the state to find food in winter

Food: seeds, insects; visits seed and suet feeders

Compare: The male Brown-headed Cowbird (p. 25) is smaller and glossier and has a brown head. Male Bronzed Cowbird (p. 29) is only slightly smaller, but more iridescent. The bold red-and-yellow epaulets distinguish the male Red-winged from other blackbirds.

Stan's Notes: One of the most widespread and numerous birds in Arizona. Found around marshes, wetlands, lakes and rivers. Flocks with as many as 10,000 birds have been reported. Males arrive before the females and sing to defend their territory. The male repeats his call from the top of a cattail while showing off his red-and-yellow shoulder patches. The female chooses a mate and often builds her nest over shallow water in a thick stand of cattails. The male can be aggressive when defending the nest. Red-winged Blackbirds feed mostly on seeds in spring and fall, and insects throughout the summer.

female
p. 163

male

Brewer's Blackbird
Euphagus cyanocephalus

YEAR-ROUND
WINTER

Size:	9" (22.5 cm)
Male:	Overall glossy black, shining green in direct light. Head more purple than green. Bright-white or pale-yellow eyes. Winter plumage can be dull gray to black.
Female:	similar to male, only overall grayish brown, most have dark eyes
Juvenile:	similar to female
Nest:	cup; female builds; 1–2 broods per year
Eggs:	4–6; gray with brown markings
Incubation:	12–14 days; female incubates
Fledging:	13–14 days; female and male feed young
Migration:	non-migrator to partial migrator in Arizona
Food:	insects, seeds, fruit
Compare:	Male Great-tailed Grackle (p. 45) is larger and has a very long tail. The male Brown-headed Cowbird (p. 25) is smaller and has a brown head. The male Bronzed Cowbird (p. 29) has red eyes. Male Red-winged Blackbird (p. 35) has red-and-yellow shoulder marks.

Stan's Notes: Common blackbird often found in association with agricultural lands and seen in open areas such as wet pastures, mountain meadows. Male and some females are easily identified by their bright, nearly white eyes. It is a common cowbird host, usually nesting in a shrub, small tree or directly on the ground. Prefers to nest in small colonies of up to 20 pairs. Gathers in large flocks with cowbirds, Red-wingeds and other blackbirds to migrate. It is expanding its range in North America.

female
p. 175

male

Yellow-headed Blackbird

Xanthocephalus xanthocephalus

SUMMER
MIGRATION
WINTER

Size: 9–11" (23–28 cm)

Male: Large black bird with a lemon-yellow head, breast and nape of neck. Black mask and gray bill. White wing patches.

Female: similar to male but slightly smaller with a brown body and dull-yellow head and chest

Juvenile: similar to female

Nest: cup; female builds; 2 broods per year

Eggs: 3–5; greenish white with brown markings

Incubation: 11–13 days; female incubates

Fledging: 9–12 days; female feeds the young

Migration: complete, to southern Arizona and Mexico

Food: insects, seeds; will come to ground feeders

Compare: The male Red-winged Blackbird (p. 35) is smaller and has red-and-yellow patches on its wings. Look for the bright-yellow head to identify the male Yellow-headed.

Stan's Notes: Found around marshes, wetlands and lakes. Nests in deep water, unlike its cousin, the Red-winged Blackbird, which prefers shallow water. Usually heard before seen. Gives a raspy, low, metallic-sounding call. The male is the only large black bird with a bright-yellow head. He gives an impressive mating display, flying with his head drooped and feet and tail pointing down while steadily beating his wings. Young keep low and out of sight for up to three weeks before they start to fly. Migrates in large flocks of as many as 200 birds, often with Red-winged Blackbirds and Brown-headed Cowbirds. Flocks of mainly males return in early April; females return later. Most colonies consist of 20–100 nests.

Common Gallinule
Gallinula galeata

YEAR-ROUND

Size: 13–15" (33–38 cm)

Male: Nearly black overall with yellow-tipped red bill. Red forehead. Thin line of white along sides. Yellowish-green legs.

Female: same as male

Juvenile: same as adult, but brown with white throat and dirty-yellow legs

Nest: ground; female and male build; 1–2 broods per year

Eggs: 2–10; brown with dark markings

Incubation: 19–22 days; female and male incubate

Fledging: 40–50 days; female and male feed the young

Migration: non-migrator in Arizona

Food: insects, snails, seeds, green leaves, fruit

Compare: American Coot (p. 43) is similar in size but lacks the distinctive yellow-tipped bill and red forehead of Common Gallinule.

Stan's Notes: Also known as Mud Hen or Pond Chicken. A nearly all-black duck-like bird often seen in freshwater marshes and lakes. Walks on floating vegetation or swims while hunting for insects. Females known to lay eggs in other gallinule nests in addition to their own. Builds its nest with cattails and bulrushes and sometimes takes an old nest in a low shrub. A cooperative breeder, having young of first brood help raise young of second. Young leave nest usually within a few hours after hatching but stay with the family for a couple months. Young ride on backs of adults.

American Coot
Fulica americana

YEAR-ROUND

Size: 13–16" (33–40 cm)

Male: Gray-to-black waterbird. Duck-like white bill with a dark band near the tip and a small red patch near the eyes. Small white patch near base of tail. Green legs and feet. Red eyes.

Female: same as male

Juvenile: much paler than adults, with a gray bill

Nest: floating platform; female and male construct; 1 brood per year

Eggs: 9–12; pinkish buff with brown markings

Incubation: 21–25 days; female and male incubate

Fledging: 49–52 days; female and male feed young

Migration: non-migrator to partial migrator in Arizona; moves around to find food

Food: insects, aquatic plants

Compare: Smaller than most waterfowl, it is the only black, duck-like bird with a white bill.

Stan's Notes: Usually seen in large flocks on open water. Not a duck, as it has large lobed toes instead of webbed feet. An excellent diver and swimmer, bobbing its head as it swims. A favorite food of Bald Eagles. It is not often seen in flight, unless it's trying to escape from an eagle. To take off, it scrambles across the surface of the water, flapping its wings. Gives a unique series of creaks, groans and clicks. Anchors its floating platform nest to vegetation. Huge flocks with as many as 1,000 birds gather for migration. Migrates at night. The common name "Coot" comes from the Middle English word *coote*, which was used to describe various waterfowl. Also called Mud Hen.

female
p. 187

male

Great-tailed Grackle

Quiscalus mexicanus

YEAR-ROUND

Size: 18" (45 cm), male
15" (38 cm), female

Male: Large all-black bird with iridescent purple sheen on the head and back. Exceptionally long tail. Bright-yellow eyes.

Female: considerably smaller than the male, overall brown bird with gray-to-brown belly, light-brown-to-white eyes, eyebrows, throat and upper chest

Juvenile: similar to female

Nest: cup; female builds; 1–2 broods per year

Eggs: 3–5; greenish blue with brown markings

Incubation: 12–14 days; female incubates

Fledging: 21–23 days; female feeds young

Migration: non-migrator to partial migrator in Arizona; moves around to find food

Food: insects, fruit, seeds; comes to seed feeders

Compare: Male Brown-headed Cowbird (p. 25) lacks the long tail and has a brown head.

Stan's Notes: This is our largest grackle. It was once considered a subspecies of the Boat-tailed Grackle, which occurs in Florida and along the East and Gulf Coasts. A bird that prefers to nest near water in an open habitat. A colony nester. Males do not participate in nest building, incubation or raising young. Males rarely fight; females squabble over nest sites and materials. Several females mate with one male. They are expanding northward, moving into northern states. Western populations tend to be larger than the eastern. Song varies from population to population.

in flight

American Crow
Corvus brachyrhynchos

Size: 18" (45 cm)

Male: All-black bird with black bill, legs and feet. Can have a purple sheen in direct sunlight.

Female: same as male

Juvenile: same as adult

Nest: platform; female builds; 1 brood per year

Eggs: 4–6; bluish to olive-green with brown marks

Incubation: 18 days; female incubates

Fledging: 28–35 days; female and male feed the young

Migration: non-migrator to partial migrator; moves around to find food

Food: fruit, insects, mammals, fish, carrion; will come to seed and suet feeders

Compare: Chihuahuan Raven (p. 49) and Common Raven (p. 51) are similar, but they have a larger bill and have shaggy throat feathers. Crow's call is higher than the raspy, low calls of ravens. Crow has a squared tail. Ravens have a wedge-shaped tail, apparent in flight.

Stan's Notes: One of the most recognizable birds in Arizona. More common than its cousins, the ravens. Imitates other birds and human voices. One of the smartest of all birds and very social, often entertaining itself by provoking chases with other birds. Eats roadkill but is rarely hit by vehicles. Can live as long as 20 years. Often reuses its nest every year if it's not taken over by a Great Horned Owl. Unmated birds, known as helpers, help to raise the young. Extended families roost together at night, dispersing daily to hunt. Cannot soar on thermals; flaps constantly and glides downward.

in flight

YEAR-ROUND

Chihuahuan Raven
Corvus cryptoleucus

Size: 20" (50 cm)

Male: Large all-black bird with a large black bill. Long bristle-like feathers cover more than half the length of the bill. Slightly shaggy throat feathers. Black legs and feet.

Female: same as male

Juvenile: similar to adult, but color of feathers on the neck is sometimes lighter

Nest: cup; female builds; 1 brood per year

Eggs: 5–7; gray to green with brown markings

Incubation: 19–21 days; female and male incubate

Fledging: 28–30 days; female and male feed young

Migration: non-migrator

Food: seeds, leaves, insects, fruit, small mammals

Compare: Common Raven (p. 51) is very similar, but it is larger and has a larger and longer bill. The American Crow (p. 47) lacks the shaggy throat and has a smaller bill.

Stan's Notes: Often confused with crows and other ravens. Usually found in open, flat regions. Known to cache food. Male performs an impressive aerial display, soaring and tumbling, then standing in front of female with neck feathers fluffed. Builds a loose cup nest of sticks and lines it with hair and dry grass. Nest is usually solitary in a tree. Will reuse its nest several years in a row. Often breeds late in the season, presumably to time hatching with the flush of insects after the rainy season. Forms large flocks of up to several hundred after young leave the nest and throughout the winter.

in flight

Common Raven
Corvus corax

YEAR-ROUND

Size: 22–27" (56–69 cm)

Male: Large all-black bird with a shaggy beard of feathers on throat and chin. Large black bill. Large wedge-shaped tail, best seen in flight.

Female: same as male

Juvenile: same as adult

Nest: platform; female and male construct; 1 brood per year

Eggs: 4–6; pale green with brown markings

Incubation: 18–21 days; female incubates

Fledging: 38–44 days; female and male feed the young

Migration: non-migrator to partial migrator; will move around to find food

Food: insects, fruit, small animals, carrion

Compare: Chihuahuan Raven (p. 49) is similar but smaller. American Crow (p. 47) is smaller and lacks the shaggy throat feathers. Low raspy call, compared with the higher-pitched call of the Chihuahuan Raven and American Crow. Glides on flat, outstretched wings, unlike Crow's slightly V-shaped wings.

Stan's Notes: Considered by some people to be the smartest of all birds. Known for its aerial acrobatics and long swooping dives. Soars on wind without flapping, like a raptor. Sometimes scavenges with crows and gulls. A cooperative hunter that often communicates the location of a good source of food to other ravens. Most start to breed at 3–4 years. Complex courtship includes grabbing bills, preening each other and cooing. Long-term pair bond. Uses the same nest site for many years. Very difficult to tell Chihuahuan Ravens and Common Ravens apart.

soaring

juvenile

drying

Turkey Vulture
Cathartes aura

YEAR-ROUND SUMMER

Size: 26–32" (66–80 cm); up to 6' wingspan

Male: Large and black with a naked red head and legs. In flight, wings are two-toned with a black leading edge and a gray trailing edge. Wing tips end in finger-like projections. Tail is long and squared. Ivory bill.

Female: same as male but slightly smaller

Juvenile: similar to adults, with a gray-to-blackish head and bill

Nest: no nest or minimal nest, on a cliff or in a cave, sometimes in a hollow tree; 1 brood per year

Eggs: 1–3; white with brown markings

Incubation: 38–41 days; female and male incubate

Fledging: 66–88 days; female and male feed the young

Migration: complete, to southern Arizona, Mexico and Central and South America

Food: carrion; parents regurgitate to feed the young

Compare: Bald Eagle (p. 81) is larger and lacks two-toned wings. Look for the obvious naked red head to identify the Turkey Vulture.

Stan's Notes: The naked head reduces the risk of feather fouling (picking up diseases) from contact with carcasses. It has a strong bill for tearing apart flesh. Unlike hawks and eagles, it has weak feet more suited for walking than grasping. One of the few birds with a developed sense of smell. Mostly mute, making only grunts and groans. Holds its wings in an upright V shape in flight. Teeters from wing tip to wing tip as it soars and hovers. Seen in trees with wings outstretched, sunning itself and drying after a rain.

SUMMER

Painted Redstart
Myioborus pictus

Size:	6" (15 cm)
Male:	Nearly all-black bird with a white patch on the wings and white outer tail feathers. A crescent-shaped white mark below the eyes. Bright-red breast and belly. Narrow, pointed black bill. Black legs and feet. Slight crest.
Female:	same as male
Juvenile:	similar to adult but lacks a red belly
Nest:	cup; female builds; 1–2 broods per year
Eggs:	3–4; creamy white with brown markings
Incubation:	13–14 days; female incubates
Fledging:	11–13 days; female and male feed young
Migration:	complete, to Mexico
Food:	insects
Compare:	Black Phoebe (p. 59) is larger and has a white belly. Look for the red belly and breast of Painted Redstart to help identify.

Stan's Notes: A very active bird of woodlands with water nearby. Constantly flits from branch to branch in search of insects. Leans forward, spreads tail and flares wings, flashing its black and white colors. This behavior presumably helps individuals visually locate each other while feeding. Males arrive at breeding sites about one week before the females. Male performs an erratic courtship flight, then chases female. Female builds a cup nest under an overhanging riverbank or cliff. Female broods the young, but both parents feed them. Young of the first clutch disperse quickly while adults start a second clutch. A summer resident, but some stay in Arizona during winter.

White-throated Swift

Aeronautes saxatilis

YEAR-ROUND
SUMMER

Size: 6½" (16 cm)

Male: Black with a white chin, chest and sides of rump. White trailing edge on the length of the first half of wings. Long narrow wings and long thin tail, as seen in flight.

Female: same as male

Juvenile: similar to adult

Nest: cup, in a cavity or crevice; female builds; 1 brood per year

Eggs: 4–5; white without markings

Incubation: 20–27; female and male incubate

Fledging: unknown number of days before fledging; female and male feed the young

Migration: complete, to southern Arizona, Mexico and Central America

Food: insects

Compare: Violet-green Swallow (p. 321), which is similar but not related, is entirely white beneath, compared with the narrow white band on the belly of White-throated Swift.

Stan's Notes: A common bird of rocky canyons in elevations from 5,500 to 8,200 feet (1,700 to 2,500 m). Almost always flying, it feeds, bathes and even mates while flying. Pairs press together and spin down through air, then break apart. Flies in groups, giving twittering calls. Returns in April. Doesn't nest until summer, when more insects are available to feed to young. Carries food to the young in an expandable throat pouch. Nests in small colonies, constructing cup-shaped nests in rock crevices. Like other swifts, uses its saliva to glue feathers and vegetation into a cup that it seals to the rock.

Black Phoebe
Sayornis nigricans

Size: 7" (18 cm)

Male: Black head, neck, breast and back with a white belly and undertail. Long narrow tail. Dark eyes, bill and legs. Can raise and lower its small crest.

Female: same as male

Juvenile: similar to adult, brown-to-tan wing bars

Nest: cup; female builds; 1–2 broods per year

Eggs: 3–6; white without markings

Incubation: 15–17 days; female incubates

Fledging: 14–21 days; female and male feed young

Migration: partial migrator to non-migrator; will move around after breeding to find food

Food: insects

Compare: Distinctive black-and-white pattern makes identification easy. Watch for tail to pump up and down very quickly when perched. The male Vermilion Flycatcher (p. 339) is crimson and black. Say's Phoebe (p. 261) has a pale-orange belly and gray head.

Stan's Notes: Often seen in shrubby areas near water. Feeds mostly on insects near the surface of water. In the winter it feeds on insects near the ground. Like other flycatchers, perches on thin branches, flies out to snatch a passing insect and returns to perch. Pumps or bobs tail up and down quickly while perching. Male performs an aerial song and flight with a slow descent to attract a mate. Female builds shallow nest of mud, adhered to rocks or bridges, lined with hair and grass. Often uses same nest or location for several years.

male

female

YEAR-ROUND

Ladder-backed Woodpecker
Dryobates scalaris

Size: 7" (18 cm)

Male: Horizontal black-and-white zebra stripes on back, wings and tail. Tan breast and belly with black spots. Red crown. Black eye stripe and mustache mark. Dark bill.

Female: same as male, but lacks a red crown

Juvenile: similar to female

Nest: cavity; female and male excavate, then use wood chips to line hole; 1 brood per year

Eggs: 2–4; white without markings

Incubation: 13–15 days; female and male incubate

Fledging: 14–16 days; female and male feed young

Migration: non-migrator

Food: insects, fruit

Compare: Gila Woodpecker (p. 67) is larger and has a brown head. Hairy Woodpecker (p. 65) lacks zebra striping on the back.

Stan's Notes: Less common than other woodpeckers of arid desert scrub. Often probes for insects and larvae or feeds on cactus fruit. Male often feeds closer to ground than female; jumping to the ground to grab an insect or pecking at the base of shrubs and trees. Female feeds higher up and probes less, pulling bugs from leaves or cracks in bark. A sharp "peek" call and short spurt of drumming. Will drum on a log or tree to advertise territory ownership. Nests in dead branches of mesquite or saguaro cactus. Sometimes will excavate a cavity in a wooden post, yucca plant or utility pole. Common name comes from the ladder-like black-and-white stripes.

male

female

Red-naped Sapsucker

Sphyrapicus nuchalis

YEAR-ROUND
SUMMER
WINTER

Size: 8½" (22 cm)

Male: Black-and-white pattern on the back in two rows. Red forehead, chin and nape of neck.

Female: same as male, but has a white chin and more white on the back

Juvenile: brown version of adults, lacking any of the red markings

Nest: cavity; female and male excavate; 1 brood per year

Eggs: 3–7; pale white without markings

Incubation: 12–13 days; female and male incubate

Fledging: 25–29 days; female and male feed young

Migration: complete, to southern Arizona, Mexico, Central America; non-migrator in a small part of Arizona

Food: insects, tree sap; will visit feeders

Compare: The Lewis's Woodpecker (p. 325) lacks the black-and-white pattern of the Red-naped.

Stan's Notes: Closely related to the Yellow-bellied Sapsucker of the eastern U.S. Often associated with aspen, cottonwood and willow trees, nearly always nesting in aspen trees where they are present. Creates several horizontal rows of holes in a tree from which sap oozes. A wide variety of birds and animals use the sap wells that sapsuckers drill. Sapsuckers can't suck sap as their name implies; instead they lap up the sap and eat the insects attracted to it. Some females lack the white chin that helps to differentiate the sexes.

male

female

YEAR-ROUND

Hairy Woodpecker
Leuconotopicus villous

Size: 9" (23 cm)

Male: Black-and-white woodpecker with a white belly. Black wings with rows of white spots. White stripe down the back. Long black bill. Red mark on the back of the head.

Female: same as male but lacks the red mark

Juvenile: grayer version of the female

Nest: cavity with an oval entrance hole; female and male excavate; 1 brood per year

Eggs: 3–6; white without markings

Incubation: 11–15 days; female incubates during the day, male incubates at night

Fledging: 28–30 days; male and female feed the young

Migration: non-migrator; moves around in winter to find food

Food: insects, nuts, seeds; comes to seed and suet feeders

Compare: Ladder-backed Woodpecker (p. 61) has zebra-like stripes. The Gila Woodpecker (p. 67) has a brown head and fine horizontal barring on its back. Look for Hairy Woodpecker's long bill.

Stan's Notes: A common bird in wooded backyards. Announces its arrival with a sharp chirp before landing on feeders. Responsible for eating many destructive forest insects. Uses its barbed tongue to extract insects from trees. Tiny, bristle-like feathers at the base of the bill protect the nostrils from wood dust. Drums on hollow logs, branches or stovepipes in spring to announce territory. Prefers to excavate nest cavities in live aspen trees. Makes short flights from tree to tree.

male

female

YEAR-ROUND

Gila Woodpecker
Melanerpes uropygialis

Size: 9" (22.5 cm)

Male: Fine pattern of black-and-white horizontal barring on the back, wings and tail. A light brown head, chest and belly. Red cap. Long dark bill. Dark eyes. Black barring on white rump. White wrist mark, seen in flight.

Female: same as male, but lacks the red cap and has a yellow wash to belly

Juvenile: similar to female

Nest: cavity; female and male excavate in cactus; 1–3 broods (3 if food is abundant) per year

Eggs: 3–4; white without markings

Incubation: 12–14 days; female and male incubate

Fledging: 10–13 days; female and male feed young

Migration: non-migrator

Food: insects, fruit, seeds

Compare: Northern Flicker (p. 181) has brown-and-black horizontal barring on the back. Acorn Woodpecker (p. 69) has an all-black back. Ladder-backed Woodpecker (p. 61) has black markings on head. Gila lacks the all-white rump of many woodpecker species.

Stan's Notes: Common in semi-desert with larger cacti. Excavates cavity in a large saguaro cactus, but due to sap oozing usually does not nest in it until the following year. Defends nest from European Starlings. Old nest cavities often used by small owls and other bird species. Gives a loud, harsh "quirrrrrrr" call to other Gilas. Also has a laughing-like "gee-gee-gee-gee" call. Stores large caches of acorns.

male

female

YEAR-ROUND

Acorn Woodpecker
Melanerpes formicivorus

Size: 9" (22.5 cm)

Male: A black-and-white woodpecker with an all-black back and prominent white eyes. Red cap and nape of neck. White forehead and cheeks. White rump and tips of wings, seen in flight.

Female: same as male, but has a smaller bill and less red on head

Juvenile: similar to adult of the same sex

Nest: cavity; male and female excavate; 1 brood per year

Eggs: 3–7; white without markings

Incubation: 11–12 days; female and male incubate

Fledging: 30–32 days; female and male feed the young

Migration: non-migrator; moves around to find acorns

Food: nuts, fruit, insects, sap; comes to suet and seed feeders

Compare: Lewis's Woodpecker (p. 325) is larger and lacks the white on head and the red cap.

Stan's Notes: A woodpecker that depends upon acorns and other nuts for survival. Dead trees are very important to this species, as they are to all woodpeckers. Drills uniform holes in trees and telephone poles, where it wedges acorns and other nuts, storing them for later consumption. Unlike other woodpeckers, it lives and nests in small colonies. Colonies consist of up to 5 males, 1–2 females and up to 12 juveniles from previous years. All members help to raise the new young. This is a very vocal species, giving a loud, nasal "wheka-wheka-wheka" call.

Black-necked Stilt
Himantopus mexicanus

YEAR-ROUND
SUMMER
MIGRATION

Size: 14" (36 cm)

Male: Black-and-white with ridiculously long red-to-pink legs. Upper parts of the head, neck and back are black. Lower parts are white. Long black bill.

Female: similar to male but browner on back

Juvenile: similar to female but brown instead of black

Nest: ground; female and male construct; 1 brood per year

Eggs: 3–5; off-white with dark markings

Incubation: 22–26 days; male incubates during the day, female incubates at night

Fledging: 28–32 days; female and male feed the young

Migration: complete, to Mexico and Central and South America; non-migrator in parts of Arizona

Food: aquatic insects

Compare: Outrageous length of the red-to-pink legs makes this shorebird hard to confuse with any other.

Stan's Notes: A unique-looking bird that seems out of place in arid Arizona. Prefers shallow water ponds, often seen at wastewater treatment facilities. Nests alone or in small colonies in open areas. This very vocal bird of shallow marshes gives a "kek-kek-kek" call. Its legs are up to 10 inches (25 cm) long and may be the longest legs in the bird world in proportion to the body. Known to transport water with water-soaked belly feathers (belly-soaking) to cool eggs in hot weather. Aggressively defends its nest, eggs and young. Young leave the nest shortly after hatching.

female p. 193

male

Lesser Scaup
Aythya affinis

WINTER

Size: 16–17" (40–43 cm)

Male: Appears mostly black with bold white sides and a gray back. Chest and head look nearly black, but head appears purple with green highlights in direct sun. Bright-yellow eyes.

Female: overall brown with a dull-white patch at the base of a light-gray bill; yellow eyes

Juvenile: same as female

Nest: ground; female builds; 1 brood per year

Eggs: 8–14; olive-buff without markings

Incubation: 22–28 days; female incubates

Fledging: 45–50 days; female teaches the young to feed

Migration: complete, to southwestern states, Mexico, Central America and northern South America

Food: aquatic plants and insects

Compare: The male Ring-necked Duck (p. 75) has a bold white ring around its bill, a black back and lacks the bold white sides of the male Lesser Scaup. The white sides and gray back help identify the male Lesser Scaup.

Stan's Notes: A common diving duck. Often seen in large flocks on lakes, ponds and sewage lagoons. Submerges completely to feed on the bottom (unlike dabbling ducks, which tip forward to reach the bottom). The male leaves the female when she starts incubating eggs. Egg quantity (clutch size) increases with the female's age. Has an interesting babysitting arrangement: groups of young (crèches) are tended by one to three adult females. A winter resident, it doesn't breed in Arizona.

female
p. 195

male

Ring-necked Duck
Aythya collaris

Size: 16–19" (41–48 cm)

Male: Striking black duck with light-gray-to-white sides. Blue bill with a bold white ring and a thinner ring at the base. Peaked head with a sloped forehead.

Female: brown with darker-brown back and crown, light-brown sides, gray face, white eye-ring, white ring around the bill, and peaked head

Juvenile: similar to female

Nest: ground; female builds; 1 brood per year

Eggs: 8–10; olive-gray to brown without markings

Incubation: 26–27 days; female incubates

Fledging: 49–56 days; female teaches the young to feed

Migration: complete migrator, to southwestern states, Mexico and Central America

Food: aquatic plants and insects

Compare: Similar size as male Lesser Scaup (p. 73), which has a gray back, unlike the black back of male Ring-necked Duck. Look for the blue bill with a bold white ring to identify the male Ring-necked Duck.

Stan's Notes: A common winter duck in Arizona. Usually in larger freshwater lakes, in small flocks or just pairs. Watch for this diving duck to dive underwater to forage for food. Springs up off the water to take flight. Flattens its crown when diving. Male gives a quick series of grating barks and grunts. Female gives high-pitched peeps. Named "Ring-necked" for its cinnamon collar, which is nearly impossible to see in the field. Also called Ring-billed Duck due to the white ring on its bill.

winter

breeding

American Avocet
Recurvirostra americana

MIGRATION

Size: 18" (45 cm)

Male: Black-and-white back, with a white belly. A long, thin upturned bill and long gray legs. Rusty-red head and neck during breeding season, gray in winter.

Female: similar to male, more strongly upturned bill

Juvenile: similar to adults, slight wash of rusty red on the neck and head

Nest: ground; female and male construct; 1 brood per year

Eggs: 3–5; light olive with brown markings

Incubation: 22–29 days; female and male incubate

Fledging: 28–35 days; female and male feed young

Migration: complete, to Mexico

Food: insects, crustaceans, aquatic vegetation, fruit

Compare: One of the few long-legged shorebirds in Arizona. Look for the rusty-red head of breeding Avocet and the long upturned bill.

Stan's Notes: A handsome, long-legged bird that prefers shallow alkaline, saline or brackish water, it is well adapted to arid western U.S. conditions. Uses its upturned bill to sweep from side to side across mud bottoms in search of insects. Both the male and female have a brood patch to incubate eggs and brood their young. Nests in loose colonies of up to 20 pairs; all members defend against intruders together. Doesn't nest in Arizona.

in flight

juvenile

YEAR-ROUND
SUMMER
MIGRATION

Black-crowned Night-Heron
Nycticorax nycticorax

Size: 22–27" (56–69 cm); up to 3½' wingspan

Male: A stocky, hunched and inactive heron with black back and crown, white belly and gray wings. Long dark bill and bright-red eyes. Short dull-yellow legs. Breeding adult has 2 long white plumes on crown.

Female: same as male

Juvenile: golden-brown head and back with white spots, streaked breast, yellow-orange eyes, brown bill

Nest: platform; female and male build; 1 brood per year

Eggs: 3–5; light blue without markings

Incubation: 24–26 days; female and male incubate

Fledging: 42–48 days; female and male feed the young

Migration: complete, to southwestern states, Mexico and Central America; non-migrator in parts of Arizona

Food: fish, aquatic insects

Compare: A perching Great Blue Heron (p. 309) looks twice the size of a Black-crowned. Look for a short-necked heron with a black back and crown.

Stan's Notes: A very secretive bird, this heron is most active near dawn and dusk (crepuscular). It hunts alone, but it nests in small colonies. Roosts in trees during the day. Often squawks if disturbed from the daytime roost. Often seen being harassed by other herons during days.

soaring

juvenile

soaring juvenile

Bald Eagle
Haliaeetus leucocephalus

Size: 31–37" (79–94 cm); up to 7½' wingspan

Male: White head and tail contrast sharply with the dark-brown-to-black body and wings. Large, curved yellow bill and yellow feet.

Female: same as male but larger

Juvenile: dark brown with white speckles and spots on the body and wings; gray bill

Nest: massive platform, usually in a tree; female and male build; 1 brood per year

Eggs: 2–3; off-white without markings

Incubation: 34–36 days; female and male incubate

Fledging: 75–90 days; female and male feed the young

Migration: partial to complete; to southwestern states

Food: fish, carrion, birds (mainly ducks)

Compare: The Golden Eagle (p. 221) and Turkey Vulture (p. 53) lack the white head and white tail of adult Bald Eagle. The juvenile Golden Eagle (p. 221), with its white wrist marks and white base of tail, is similar to the juvenile Bald Eagle.

Stan's Notes: Nearly became extinct due to DDT poisoning and illegal killing. Returns to the same nest each year, adding more sticks and enlarging it to huge proportions, at times up to 1,000 pounds (450 kg). In their midair mating ritual, one eagle flips upside down and locks talons with another. Both tumble, then break apart to continue flight. Not uncommon for juveniles to perform this mating ritual even though they have not reached breeding age. Long-term pair bond but will switch mates when not successful at reproducing. Juveniles attain the white head and tail at 4–5 years of age. Winter resident except for a few scattered locations.

soaring

juvenile

YEAR-ROUND

California Condor
Gymnogyps californianus

Size: 44–46" (112–117 cm); up to 9½' wingspan

Male: Black with splayed "fingertips" on wings and white wing linings, as seen in flight. Ruffle of feathers around neck. Orange-to-red head. Small dark patch between eyes. Short tail.

Female: same as male

Juvenile: similar to adult, but gray head and lacks the white wing linings

Nest: no nest; lays egg on a coarse gravel bed on cave floor; 0–1 brood per year

Eggs: 1; pale green without markings

Incubation: 42–50 days; female and male incubate

Fledging: 160–180 days; female and male feed young

Migration: non-migrator to partial; moves around in winter to find food

Food: carrion

Compare: Turkey Vulture (p. 53) is smaller with gray trailing edges of wings. The Golden Eagle (p. 221) is smaller and has a white base of tail. Most California Condors in the wild are marked with numbered, colored wing tags.

Stan's Notes: The largest flying bird in North America. Can soar to 15,000 feet (4,575 m). A vulture, mistaken for small aircraft. Slow wingbeats. Usually silent, will hiss if approached at nest. Matures at 6–7 years. Long-term pair bond. Most breed every other year. Presumed to live 40 years, perhaps up to 70. Has weaker feet than eagles and hawks. Nearly extinct in the 1980s. The remaining wild birds were caught and put into a captive breeding program. Young were released into the wild. Populations are slowly increasing.

male

female
p. 119

Indigo Bunting
Passerina cyanea

Size: 5½" (14 cm)

Male: Vibrant-blue finch-like bird. Dark markings scattered on wings and tail.

Female: light brown with faint markings

Juvenile: similar to female

Nest: cup; female builds; 2 broods per year

Eggs: 3–4; pale blue without markings

Incubation: 12–13 days; female incubates

Fledging: 10–11 days; female feeds the young

Migration: complete, to Mexico, Central America and South America

Food: insects, seeds, fruit; will visit seed feeders

Compare: The male Western Bluebird (p. 95) is larger and has a rust-red chest. Male Mountain Bluebird (p. 93) has a thin black bill and white lower belly.

Stan's Notes: Seen along woodland edges and in parks and yards, feeding on insects. Comes to seed feeders early in spring, before insects are plentiful. Usually only the males are noticed. The male often sings from treetops to attract a mate. The female is quiet. Actually a gray bird, without blue pigment in its feathers: like Blue Jays and other blue birds, sunlight is refracted within the structure of the feathers, making them appear blue. Plumage is iridescent in direct sun, duller in shade. Molts in spring to acquire body feathers with gray tips, which quickly wear off, revealing the bright-blue plumage. Molts in fall and appears like the female during winter. Migrates at night in flocks of 5–10 birds. Males return before the females and juveniles, often to the nest site of the preceding year. Juveniles move to within a mile of their birth site.

female
p. 121

male

SUMMER
MIGRATION
WINTER

Lazuli Bunting
Passerina amoena

Size: 5½" (14 cm)

Male: A turquoise-blue head, neck, back and tail. Cinnamon chest with cinnamon extending down flanks slightly. White belly. Two bold white wing bars. Non-breeding male has a spotty blue head and back.

Female: overall grayish brown, warm-brown breast, a light wash of blue on wings and tail, gray throat, light-gray belly and 2 narrow white wing bars

Juvenile: similar to adult of the same sex

Nest: cup; female builds; 2–3 broods per year

Eggs: 3–5; pale blue without markings

Incubation: 11–13 days; female incubates

Fledging: 10–12 days; female and male feed young

Migration: complete, to Mexico; a few winter in far southeastern Arizona

Food: insects, seeds

Compare: The male Indigo Bunting (p. 85) lacks the male Lazuli's multicolored plumage. Male Western Bluebird (p. 95) is darker blue. Male Blue Grosbeak (p. 91) has chestnut wing bars and lacks a white belly.

Stan's Notes: More common in shrublands in Arizona. Does not like dense forests. Strong association with water, such as rivers and streams. Gathers in small flocks and tends to move up in elevations after breeding to hunt for insects and look for seeds. Males sing from short shrubs and scrubby areas to attract females. Rarely perches on tall trees. Each male has his own unique combination of notes to produce his "own" song.

Barn Swallow
Hirundo rustica

Size: 7" (18 cm)

Male: Sleek swallow. Blue-black back, cinnamon belly and reddish-brown chin. White spots on a long, deeply forked tail.

Female: same as male but with a whitish belly

Juvenile: similar to adults, with a tan belly and chin, and shorter tail

Nest: cup; female and male build; 2 broods per year

Eggs: 4–5; white with brown markings

Incubation: 13–17 days; female incubates

Fledging: 18–23 days; female and male feed the young

Migration: complete, to South America

Food: insects (prefers beetles, wasps, flies)

Compare: Cliff Swallow (p. 123) and Violet-green Swallow (p. 321) are smaller and lack a distinctive, deeply forked tail. Violet-green Swallow is green with a white face. Look for Barn Swallow's deeply forked tail.

Stan's Notes: Seen in wetlands, farms, suburban yards and parks. Of the seven swallow species regularly found in Arizona, this is the only one with a deeply forked tail. Unlike other swallows, it rarely glides in flight. Usually flies low over land or water. Drinks as it flies, skimming water, or will sip water droplets on wet leaves. Bathes while flying through rain or sprinklers. Gives a twittering warble, followed by a mechanical sound. Builds a mud nest with up to 1,000 beak-loads of mud. Nests on barns and houses, under bridges and in other sheltered places. Often nests in colonies of 4–6 birds; sometimes nests alone.

female
p. 139

male

Blue Grosbeak
Passerina caerulea

Size: 7" (18 cm)

Male: Overall blue bird with 2 chestnut wing bars. Large gray-to-silver bill. Black around base of bill.

Female: overall brown with darker wings and tail, 2 tan wing bars, large gray-to-silver bill

Juvenile: similar to female

Nest: cup; female builds; 1–2 broods per year

Eggs: 3–6; pale blue without markings

Incubation: 11–12 days; female incubates

Fledging: 9–10 days; female and male feed the young

Migration: complete, to Mexico and Central America

Food: insects, seeds; will come to seed feeders

Compare: Male Lazuli Bunting (p. 87) has two bold white wing bars and a white belly. The male Indigo Bunting (p. 85) is smaller and lacks wing bars. The male Mountain and Western Bluebirds (pp. 93 and 95) are the same size, but they lack the chestnut wing bars and oversized bill.

Stan's Notes: This grosbeak returns to the state late, by early May. A bird of semi-open habitats, such as overgrown fields, riversides, woodland edges and fencerows. Visits seed feeders. The first-year males show only some blue, obtaining the full complement of blue feathers in the second winter. It has expanded northward, with overall populations increasing over the past 30–40 years.

Mountain Bluebird
Sialia currucoides

YEAR-ROUND
WINTER

Size: 7" (18 cm)

Male: Overall sky-blue bird with a darker blue head, back, wings and tail. White lower belly. Thin black bill.

Female: similar to male, but paler with a nearly gray head and chest and a whitish belly

Juvenile: similar to adult of the same sex

Nest: cavity, old woodpecker cavity, wooden nest box; female builds; 1–2 broods per year

Eggs: 4–6; pale blue without markings

Incubation: 13–14 days; female incubates

Fledging: 22–23 days; female and male feed young

Migration: non-migrator to partial migrator, to southern Arizona and Mexico

Food: insects, fruit

Compare: Western Bluebird (p. 95) is similar, but it is a darker blue and has a rusty red chest. Male Indigo Bunting (p. 85) is smaller and lacks a white lower belly. Male Blue Grosbeak (p. 91) has chestnut wing bars and an oversized bill.

Stan's Notes: Common in open mountainous country, nesting in half of Arizona. Main diet is insects. Due to conservation of suitable nesting sites (dead trees with cavities and man-made nest boxes), populations have increased over the past 40 years. Like other bluebirds, Mountain Bluebirds take well to nest boxes and tolerate close contact with people. Female sits on baby birds (brood) for up to six days after the eggs hatch. Young imprint on their first nest box or cavity and then choose a similar type of box or cavity throughout their life.

Western Bluebird
Sialia mexicana

YEAR-ROUND WINTER

Size: 7" (18 cm)

Male: Deep blue head, neck, throat, back, wings and tail. Rusty-red chest and flanks.

Female: similar to male, only duller with a gray head

Juvenile: similar to female, with a speckled chest

Nest: cavity, old woodpecker cavity, wooden nest box; female builds; 1–2 broods per year

Eggs: 4–6; pale blue without markings

Incubation: 13–14 days; female incubates

Fledging: 22–23 days; female and male feed young

Migration: non-migrator to partial migrator, to southwestern states and Mexico

Food: insects, fruit

Compare: The Mountain Bluebird (p. 93) is similar but lacks the rusty-red breast. Male Lazuli Bunting (p. 87) is smaller and has white wing bars. Male Blue Grosbeak (p. 91) is the same size but has chestnut wing bars and an oversized bill.

Stan's Notes: Not as common as the Mountain Bluebird. Found in a variety of habitats, from agricultural land to clear-cuts. Requires a cavity for nesting. Competes with starlings for nest cavities. Like the Mountain Bluebird, it uses nest boxes, which are responsible for the stable populations. A courting male will fly in front of the female, spread his wings and tail, and perch next to her. Often goes in and out of its nest box or cavity as if to say, "Look inside." Male may offer food to the female to establish a pair bond.

Pinyon Jay
Gymnorhinus cyanocephalus

Size: 11" (28 cm)

Male: A short-tailed dull-blue jay. Head is darker blue than rest of body. Faint white streaks on chin. Long, pointed black bill. Black legs.

Female: same as male

Juvenile: overall gray with blue highlights

Nest: cup; female and male construct; 1–2 broods per year

Eggs: 4–5; blue, green, gray or white with brown markings

Incubation: 16–17 days; female incubates

Fledging: 19–21 days; female and male feed young

Migration: non-migrator; moves around to find food

Food: seeds, insects, fruit

Compare: The Woodhouse's Scrub-Jay (p. 101) has a white chest and belly. Steller's Jay (p. 99) has a black head and crest. Mexican Jay (p. 103) has a gray chest and belly.

Stan's Notes: Highly specialized jay, usually seen near pinyon pine trees. Gathers nuts from pinyon cones, storing them in large caches often on the ground. An important seed disperser, with forgotten caches sprouting into new trees. Can breed in late winter in years with abundant seed production. Gregarious, it breeds in colonies of up to 50 pairs. Starts breeding at age 3. Mates are often the same age and stay together for years. In winter, flocks of up to several hundred gather to roost and find food and move on when supplies are low. Has a soft flight song of, "hoyi-hoyi-hoyi-hoyi." Often walks rather than hops, like most other jays. Closely related to Clark's Nutcracker.

YEAR-ROUND

Steller's Jay
Cyanocitta stelleri

Size: 11" (28 cm)

Male: Dark-blue wings, tail and belly. Black head, nape of the neck and chest. Large, pointed black crest on head that can be lifted at will. Distinctive white streaks on forehead and just above eyes.

Female: same as male

Juvenile: similar to adult

Nest: cup; female and male construct; 1 brood per year

Eggs: 3–5; pale green with brown markings

Incubation: 14–16 days; female incubates

Fledging: 16–18 days; female and male feed the young

Migration: non-migrator; moves around to find food

Food: insects, berries, seeds; will visit seed feeders

Compare: The Woodhouse's Scrub-Jay (p. 101) and Mexican Jay (p. 103) are the same size, but they lack the black head and crest of the Steller's Jay.

Stan's Notes: Common resident of foothills and lower mountains from 6,000 to 8,000 feet (1,850 to 2,450 m). Usually only found in conifer forests. Thought to mate for life, rarely dispersing far, usually breeding within 10 miles (16 km) of the place of birth. Several subspecies found throughout the Rockies. The Arizona form has a black crest with distinct white streaks, while others lack white markings. Named after the Arctic explorer Georg W. Steller, who is said to have first recorded the bird on the coast of Alaska in 1741.

YEAR-ROUND

Woodhouse's Scrub-Jay
Aphelocoma woodhouseii

Size: 11" (28 cm)

Male: Blue head, wings, tail and breast band. Brownish patch on back. Dull white chin, breast and belly. Very long tail.

Female: same as male

Juvenile: similar to adult, overall gray with light-blue wings and tail

Nest: cup; female and male construct; 1 brood per year

Eggs: 3–6; pale green with red-brown markings

Incubation: 15–17 days; female incubates

Fledging: 18–20 days; female and male feed young

Migration: non-migrator; moves around to find food in winter

Food: insects, seeds, fruit; comes to seed feeders

Compare: The closely related Mexican Jay (p. 103) is slightly larger, lighter blue and lacks a brownish patch on the back. Steller's Jay (p. 99) is similar in size but lacks the black head and the crest. Pinyon Jay (p. 97) has a light-blue chest and belly.

Stan's Notes: A tame bird of urban areas that visits feeders. Forms a long-term pair bond, with the male feeding female before and during incubation. Young of a pair remain close by for up to a couple years, helping parents raise subsequent brothers and sisters. Caches food by burying it for later consumption. Likely serves as a major distributor of oaks and pines by not returning to eat the seeds it buried.

YEAR-ROUND

Mexican Jay
Aphelocoma wollweberi

Size: 11½" (29 cm)

Male: Mostly blue with plain gray chest and belly. Gray can extend to upper back. Large black bill. Black legs.

Female: same as male

Juvenile: similar to adult, gray head, neck and back, black-tipped yellow bill until 2 years old

Nest: cup; female and male build; 1 brood per year

Eggs: 4–5; pale green without markings

Incubation: 16–18 days; female incubates

Fledging: 24–26 days; female and male feed young

Migration: non-migrator

Food: fruit, insects, seeds, reptiles

Compare: Woodhouse's Scrub-Jay (p. 101) is darker blue and has a brownish patch on the back and a white chin. Steller's Jay (p. 99) is slightly smaller and has a black head and crest. Pinyon Jay (p. 97) has a light-blue chest and belly.

Stan's Notes: In the U.S. this jay occurs only in Arizona and parts of New Mexico and Texas. The Arizona variety is larger and lighter blue than the Texas version. Often travels around in large groups of mostly family members in search of acorns, one of its favorite foods. During courtship, male displays to female, circling her with tail and wings tilted toward her. Usually only a couple dominant females of an extended family group breed each year. The remainder of the flock help raise the young. Closely related to scrub-jays. Formerly called Gray-breasted Jay.

male

female

Belted Kingfisher

Megaceryle alcyon

WINTER

Size: 12–14" (30–36 cm)

Male: Blue with white belly, blue-gray chest band, and black wing tips. Ragged crest moves up and down at will. Large head. Long, thick, black bill. White spot by eyes. Red-brown eyes.

Female: same as male but with rusty flanks and a rusty chest band below the blue-gray band

Juvenile: similar to female

Nest: cavity; female and male excavate in a bank of a river, lake or cliff; 1 brood per year

Eggs: 6–7; white without markings

Incubation: 23–24 days; female and male incubate

Fledging: 23–24 days; female and male feed the young

Migration: complete migrator, to southwestern states, Mexico and Central and South America

Food: small fish

Compare: Woodhouse's Scrub-Jay (p. 101) is smaller. The Belted Kingfisher is rarely found away from water.

Stan's Notes: Usually found at the bank of a river, lake or large stream. Perches on a branch near water, dives in headfirst to catch a small fish, then returns to the branch to feed. Parents drop dead fish into the water to teach their young to dive. Can't pass bones through its digestive tract; regurgitates bone pellets after meals. Loud call that sounds like a machine gun. Mates know each other by their calls. Digs a tunnel up to 4 feet (about 1 m) long to a nest chamber. Small white patches on dark wing tips flash during flight.

Chipping Sparrow
Spizella passerina

Size: 5" (13 cm)

Male: Small gray-brown sparrow with clear-gray chest. Rusty crown. White eyebrows and thin black eye line. Thin gray-black bill. Two faint wing bars.

Female: same as male

Juvenile: similar to adults, with streaking on the chest; lacks a rusty crown

Nest: cup; female builds; 2 broods per year

Eggs: 3–5; blue-green with brown markings

Incubation: 11–14 days; female incubates

Fledging: 10–12 days; female and male feed the young

Migration: complete to southern Arizona, Mexico and Central America; non-migratory in southeastern Arizona

Food: insects, seeds; will come to ground feeders

Compare: The Lark Sparrow (p. 133) is larger and has a white chest and central spot. Song Sparrow (p. 115) and female House Finch (p. 111) have heavily streaked chests. Fox Sparrow (p. 137) is larger and lacks the rusty crown.

Stan's Notes: A common garden or yard bird, often seen feeding on dropped seeds beneath feeders. Gathers in large family groups to feed in preparation for migration. Migrates at night in flocks of 20–30 birds. The common name comes from the male's fast "chip" call. Often is just called Chippy. Builds nest low in dense shrubs and almost always lines it with animal hair. Comfortable with people, allowing you to approach closely before it flies away.

Pine Siskin
Spinus pinus

YEAR-ROUND WINTER

Size: 5" (13 cm)

Male: Small brown finch with heavy streaking on the back, breast and belly. Yellow wing bars. Yellow at the base of tail. Thin bill.

Female: similar to male, with less yellow

Juvenile: similar to adult, with a light-yellow tinge over the breast and chin

Nest: cup; female builds; 2 broods

Eggs: 3–4; greenish blue with brown markings

Incubation: 12–13 days; female incubates

Fledging: 14–15 days; female and male feed the young

Migration: non-migrator; moves around the United States in search of food

Food: seeds, insects; will come to seed feeders

Compare: Female House Finch (p. 111) lacks any yellow. The female American Goldfinch (p. 357) has white wing bars and lacks streaks. Look for the yellow wing bars to identify the Pine Siskin.

Stan's Notes: A nesting resident, it is usually considered a winter finch because it is more visible in the non-nesting season, when it gathers in flocks, moves around the state and visits bird feeders. Seen in flocks of up to 20 birds, often with other finch species. Will come to thistle feeders. Gives a series of high-pitched, wheezy calls. Also gives a wheezing twitter. Breeds in small groups. Builds nest toward the end of coniferous branches, where needles are dense, helping to conceal. Nests are often only a few feet apart. Male feeds the female during incubation. Juveniles lose the yellow tint by late summer of their first year.

male
p. 337

female

House Finch
Haemorhous mexicanus

YEAR-ROUND

Size:	5" (13 cm)
Female:	Plain brown with heavy streaking on a white chest.
Male:	red-to-orange face, throat, chest and rump, streaked belly and wings, brown cap, brown marking behind the eyes
Juvenile:	similar to female
Nest:	cup, occasionally in a cavity; female builds; 2 broods per year
Eggs:	4–5; pale blue, lightly marked
Incubation:	12–14 days; female incubates
Fledging:	15–19 days; female and male feed the young
Migration:	non-migrator to partial migrator; will move around to find food
Food:	seeds, fruit, leaf buds; visits seed feeders and feeders that offer grape jelly
Compare:	Pine Siskin (p. 109) is similar but has yellow wing bars and a smaller bill. The female American Goldfinch (p. 357) has a clear chest and while wing bars.

Stan's Notes: Can be a common bird at your feeders. A very social bird, visiting feeders in small flocks. Likes to nest in hanging flower baskets. Male sings a loud, cheerful warbling song. Historically it occurred from the Pacific Coast to the Rockies, with only a few reaching the eastern side. Now found throughout the country. Suffers from a disease that causes the eyes to crust, resulting in blindness and death.

House Wren
Troglodytes aedon

Size: 5" (13 cm)

Male: All-brown bird with lighter-brown markings on the wings and tail. Slightly curved brown bill. Often holds tail upward.

Female: same as male

Juvenile: same as adult

Nest: cavity; female and male line just about any nest cavity; 2 broods per year

Eggs: 4–6; tan with brown markings

Incubation: 10–13 days; female and male incubate

Fledging: 12–15 days; female and male feed the young

Migration: complete, to southern Arizona and Mexico

Food: insects, spiders, snails

Compare: The Bewick's Wren (p. 125), Canyon Wren (p. 127) and Rock Wren (p. 129) are slightly larger. Bewick's Wren has white eyebrows. Canyon Wren has a distinctive white throat and chest and a long down-curved bill. Rock Wren has fine white speckles on the back with a light-tan belly and chest.

Stan's Notes: A prolific songster. During the mating season, sings from dawn to dusk. Seen in brushy yards, parks and woodlands and along forest edges. Easily attracted to a nest box. In spring, the male chooses several prospective nesting cavities and places a few small twigs in each. The female inspects all of them and finishes constructing the nest in the cavity of her choice. She fills the cavity with short twigs and then lines a small depression at the back with pine needles and grass. She often has trouble fitting longer twigs through the entrance hole and tries many different directions and approaches until she is successful.

Song Sparrow
Melospiza melodia

YEAR-ROUND

Size: 5–6" (13–15 cm)

Male: Common brown sparrow with heavy dark streaks on the chest coalescing into a central dark spot.

Female: same as male

Juvenile: similar to adults, with a finely streaked chest; lacks a central dark spot

Nest: cup; female builds; 2 broods per year

Eggs: 3–4; blue to green, with red-brown markings

Incubation: 12–14 days; female incubates

Fledging: 9–12 days; female and male feed the young

Migration: non-migrator in Arizona

Food: insects, seeds; only rarely comes to ground feeders with seeds

Compare: Similar to other brown sparrows. Look for the heavily streaked chest with a central dark spot to help identify the Song Sparrow.

Stan's Notes: There are many subspecies of this bird, but the dark spot in the center of the chest appears in every variety. A constant songster, repeating its loud, clear song every few minutes. The song varies from region to region but has the same basic structure. Sings from thick shrubs to defend a small territory, beginning with three notes and finishing up with a trill. A ground feeder, it will "double-scratch" with both feet at the same time to expose seeds. When the female builds a new nest for a second brood, the male often takes over feeding the first brood. Unlike many other sparrow species, Song Sparrows rarely flock together. A common host of the Brown-headed and Bronzed Cowbirds.

male
p. 245

female

pink-sided

Oregon
female

Dark-eyed Junco
Junco hyemalis

Size: 5½" (14 cm)

Female: A plump, dark-eyed bird with a tan-to-brown chest, head and back. White belly. Ivory-to-pink bill. White outer tail feathers appear like a white V in flight.

Male: round bird with gray plumage

Juvenile: similar to female, with streaking on the breast and head

Nest: cup; female and male build; 2 broods per year

Eggs: 3–5; white with reddish-brown markings

Incubation: 12–13 days; female incubates

Fledging: 10–13 days; male and female feed the young

Migration: partial to non-migrator in Arizona

Food: seeds, insects; visits ground and seed feeders

Compare: Rarely confused with any other bird. Look for the ivory-to-pink bill and small flocks feeding beneath seed feeders to help identify the female Dark-eyed Junco.

Stan's Notes: A common year-round resident and one of the most numerous wintering birds in the state and a common year-round resident in northern Arizona. Spends winters in foothills and plains, returning to higher elevations for nesting. Adheres to a rigid social hierarchy, with dominant birds chasing the less dominant birds. Look for the white outer tail feathers flashing in flight. Often seen in small flocks on the ground, where it uses its feet to simultaneously "double-scratch" to expose seeds and insects. Eats many weed seeds. Nests in a wide variety of wooded habitats in April and May. Several sub-species of Dark-eyed Junco were previously considered to be separate species (see lower insets).

female

male
p. 85

SUMMER

Indigo Bunting
Passerina cyanea

Size: 5½" (14 cm)

Female: Light-brown, finch-like bird. Faint streaking on a light-tan chest. Wings have a very faint blue cast and indistinct wing bars.

Male: vibrant blue with scattered dark markings on wings and tail

Juvenile: similar to female

Nest: cup; female builds; 2 broods per year

Eggs: 3–4; pale blue without markings

Incubation: 12–13 days; female incubates

Fledging: 10–11 days; female feeds the young

Migration: complete, to Mexico, Central America and South America

Food: insects, seeds, fruit; will visit seed feeders

Compare: Female Lazuli Bunting (p. 121) is extremely similar, but is has more-defined wing bars. Female Blue Grosbeak (p. 139) is larger and has 2 tan wing bars. The female House Finch (p. 111) has a heavily streaked chest. Female American Goldfinch (p. 357) has white wing bars. Look for the faint blue cast on the wings to help identify the female Indigo Bunting.

Stan's Notes: Seen along woodland edges and in parks and yards, feeding on insects. Comes to seed feeders early in spring, before insects are plentiful. Secretive, plain and quiet; usually only the males are noticed. The male often sings from treetops to attract a mate. Migrates at night in flocks of 5–10 birds. Males return before the females and juveniles, often to the nest site of the preceding year. Juveniles move to within a mile of their birth site.

female

male
p. 87

Lazuli Bunting
Passerina amoena

SUMMER
MIGRATION
WINTER

Size: 5½" (14 cm)

Female: Overall grayish brown with a warm brown chest, light wash of blue on wings and tail, gray throat and light-gray belly. Two narrow white wing bars.

Male: turquoise-blue head, neck, back and tail, cinnamon breast, white belly, 2 bold white wing bars

Juvenile: similar to adult of the same sex

Nest: cup; female builds; 2–3 broods per year

Eggs: 3–5; pale blue without markings

Incubation: 11–13 days; female incubates

Fledging: 10–12 days; female and male feed the young

Migration: complete, to Mexico

Food: insects, seeds

Compare: Female Indigo Bunting (p. 119) is the same size but has faint streaking on the breast and less obvious wing bars. Similar to the female Blue Grosbeak (p. 139), which is overall darker and has tan wing bars. Female Western (p. 95) and Mountain (p. 93) Bluebirds are larger and have much more blue than female Bunting.

Stan's Notes: More common in shrublands in Arizona. Doesn't like dense forests. Strong association with water, such as rivers and streams. Gathers in small flocks and tends to move up in elevations after breeding to hunt for insects and look for seeds. Has increased in population and expanded its range over the last century. Males sing from short shrubs and scrubby areas to attract females. Rarely perches on tall trees. Each male has his own unique combination of notes to produce his "own" song.

Cliff Swallow
Petrochelidon pyrrhonota

SUMMER
MIGRATION

Size: 5½" (14 cm)

Male: Uniquely patterned swallow with a dark back, wings and cap. Distinctive tan-to-rust rump, cheeks and forehead.

Female: same as male

Juvenile: similar to adult, lacks distinct patterning

Nest: gourd-shaped, made of mud; male and female build; 1–2 broods per year

Eggs: 4–6; pale white with brown markings

Incubation: 14–16 days; male and female incubate

Fledging: 21–24 days; female and male feed young

Migration: complete, to South America

Food: insects

Compare: Barn Swallow (p. 89) is larger and has a distinctive, deeply forked tail and blue back and wings. Violet-green Swallow (p. 321) is green with a bright-white face.

Stan's Notes: A common and widespread swallow species in the state. Common around bridges (especially bridges over water) and rural housing (especially in open country near cliffs). Builds a gourd-shaped nest with a funnel-like entrance pointing down. A colony nester, with many nests lined up beneath building eaves or cliff overhangs. Will carry balls of mud up to a mile to construct its nest. Many in the colony return to the same nest site each year. Not unusual to have two broods per season. If the number of nests underneath eaves becomes a problem, wait until the young have left the nests to hose off the mud.

Bewick's Wren
Thryomanes bewickii

YEAR-ROUND
WINTER

Size: 5½" (14 cm)

Male: Brown cap, back, wings and tail. Gray chest and belly. White chin and eyebrows. Long tail with white spots on edges is cocked and flits sideways. Pointed down-curved bill.

Female: same as male

Juvenile: similar to adult

Nest: cavity; female and male build nest in woodpecker hole or nest box; 2–3 broods a year

Eggs: 4–8; white with brown markings

Incubation: 12–14 days; female incubates

Fledging: 10–14 days; female and male feed young

Migration: non-migrator to partial migrator; will move around to find food

Food: insects, seeds

Compare: The House Wren (p. 113) is slightly smaller and lacks the obvious white eyebrow marks and white spots on tail. The Rock Wren (p. 129) has a gray back with white spots.

Stan's Notes: A common wren of backyards and gardens. Insects make up 97 percent of its diet, with plant seeds composing the rest. Competes with House Wrens for nesting cavities. Male will choose nesting cavities and start to build nests using small uniform-sized sticks. Female will make the final selection of a nest site and finish building. Begins breeding in March and April. Has 2–3 broods per year. Male feeds female while she incubates. Average size territory per pair is 5 acres (2 ha), which they defend all year long.

Canyon Wren
Catherpes mexicanus

YEAR-ROUND

Size: 5¾" (14.5 cm)

Male: Chestnut back, wings, belly and tail. Gray head and nape of neck. A distinctive white throat and chest. Long downward-curving bill. Tail often cocked up.

Female: same as male

Juvenile: similar to adult

Nest: crevice; male and female build; 1–2 broods per year

Eggs: 4–6; white with light-brown markings

Incubation: 14–16 days; female and male incubate

Fledging: 14–18 days; female and male feed young

Migration: non-migrator to partial; will move around to find food

Food: insects

Compare: Rock Wren (p. 129) is slightly larger and tends to be more grayish, with white chin not as prominent. House Wren (p. 113) is slightly smaller and lacks the large bill of the Canyon Wren.

Stan's Notes: An active wren, spending its entire life among rocks and cliffs. Prefers steep-sided canyons, hence its common name. Maintains winter territories, usually around running water, to hunt for winter-active insects. Territories are up to 2 acres (1 ha) in size. Nests are attached to rocks within crevices that usually have some kind of rock covering. May reuse the nest from year to year. Lives in close association with Rock Wrens (p. 129), which use scattered boulders and rocks for nesting.

Rock Wren
Salpinctes obsoletus

YEAR-ROUND

Size: 6" (15 cm)

Male: Overall grayish brown with tinges of buffy brown on tail and wings. Gray back, often finely speckled with white. Belly and breast are light tan.

Female: same as male

Juvenile: similar to adult

Nest: crevice; male and female build; 1–2 broods per year

Eggs: 4–8; white with light-brown markings

Incubation: 14–16 days; female and male incubate

Fledging: 14–18 days; female and male feed young

Migration: non-migrator in Arizona

Food: insects

Compare: Canyon Wren (p. 127) is slightly smaller, mostly chestnut brown and has a much larger and down-curved bill. House Wren (p. 113) is slightly smaller and lacks Rock Wren's white speckles on back.

Stan's Notes: Consistently uses open sunny piles of broken rocks (scree) and rock debris at cliff bases (talus slopes) for nesting. Often builds a small runway of flat stones leading up to the nest, which is usually in a rock crevice. Lives in close association with Canyon Wrens, which use steep-sided canyons for nesting. Known to also nest on prairies, where it uses dirt banks instead of rock piles. Begins nesting in May, with the female doing most of the incubating and the male feeding the female during incubation.

male

female

House Sparrow
Passer domesticus

YEAR-ROUND

Size: 6" (15 cm)

Male: Brown back with a gray belly and cap. Large black patch extending from the throat to the chest (bib). One white wing bar.

Female: slightly smaller than the male; light brown with light eyebrows; lacks a bib and white wing bar

Juvenile: similar to female

Nest: cavity; female and male build a domed cup nest within; 2–3 broods per year

Eggs: 4–6; white with brown markings

Incubation: 10–12 days; female incubates

Fledging: 14–17 days; female and male feed the young

Migration: non-migrator; moves around to find food

Food: seeds, insects, fruit; comes to seed feeders

Compare: Chipping Sparrow (p. 107) has a rusty-red crown. Look for the black bib to identify the male House Sparrow and the clear breast to help identify the female.

Stan's Notes: One of the first birdsongs heard in cities in spring. A familiar city bird, nearly always in small flocks. Also found on farms. Introduced in 1850 from Europe to Central Park in New York. Now seen throughout North America. Related to old-world sparrows; not a relative of any sparrows in the U.S. An aggressive bird that will kill young birds in order to take over the nest cavity. Uses dried grass and small scraps of plastic, paper and other materials to build an oversize, domed nest in the cavity.

Lark Sparrow
Chondestes grammacus

YEAR-ROUND
SUMMER
MIGRATION
WINTER

Size: 6½" (16 cm)

Male: All-brown bird with unique rust-red, white and black head pattern. A white breast with a central black spot. Gray rump and white edges to gray tail, as seen in flight.

Female: same as male

Juvenile: similar to adult, but no rust-red on head

Nest: cup, on the ground; female builds; 1 brood per year

Eggs: 3–6; pale white with brown markings

Incubation: 10–12 days; male and female incubate

Fledging: 10–12 days; female and male feed young

Migration: complete, to southern Arizona, coastal Mexico and Central America; non-migrator in southeastern Arizona

Food: seeds, insects

Compare: The White-crowned Sparrow (p. 135) lacks the Lark Sparrow's rust-red pattern on the head and central spot on a white chest. Chipping Sparrow (p. 107) has a similar rusty color on head, but it is smaller and lacks Lark Sparrow's white breast and central spot.

Stan's Notes: One of the larger sparrow species and one of the best songsters, also well known for its courtship strutting, chasing and lark-like flight pattern (rapid wingbeats with tail spread). A bird of open fields, pastures and prairies, found almost anywhere. Very common during migration, when large flocks congregate. Will use nest for several years if first brood is successful.

juvenile

WINTER

White-crowned Sparrow
Zonotrichia leucophrys

Size: 6½–7½" (16.5–19 cm)

Male: Brown with a gray chest and black-and-white striped crown. Small, thin, pink bill.

Female: same as male

Juvenile: similar to adults, with black and brown stripes on the head

Nest: cup; female builds; 2 broods per year

Eggs: 3–5; greenish to bluish to whitish with red-brown markings

Incubation: 11–14 days; female incubates

Fledging: 8–12 days; male and female feed the young

Migration: complete migrator, to Arizona, other southwestern states and Mexico

Food: insects, seeds, berries; visits ground feeders

Compare: The Black-throated Sparrow (p. 255) is smaller and has a large black patch on the throat. Lark Sparrow (p. 133) has a rust-red pattern on the head and a central black spot on a white breast.

Stan's Notes: A winter visitor throughout Arizona. Usually seen in groups of up to 20 birds during migration, when it can be seen feeding beneath seed feeders. This ground feeder will "double-scratch" backward with both feet simultaneously to find seeds. Nesting begins in May. The males are prolific songsters, singing in late winter while migrating north. Males arrive at the breeding grounds before the females and sing from perches to establish territory. Males take most of the responsibility for raising the young while females start their second broods. Only 9–12 days separate the broods.

Fox Sparrow
Passerella iliaca

MIGRATION
WINTER

Size: 7" (18 cm)

Male: A plump, brown sparrow with a gray head, back and rump. White chest and belly with rusty brown streaks. Rusty tail and wings.

Female: same as male

Juvenile: same as adult

Nest: cup; female builds; 2 broods per year

Eggs: 2–4; pale green with reddish markings

Incubation: 12–14 days; female incubates

Fledging: 10–11 days; male and female feed the young

Migration: complete, to southern Arizona

Food: seeds, insects; comes to ground feeders

Compare: The Spotted Towhee (p. 33) is found in similar habitats, but the male towhee has a black head and both male and female have white bellies.

Stan's Notes: One of the largest sparrows. Often alone or in small groups. Found in shrubby areas, open fields and backyards. Comes to ground feeders and seen underneath seed feeders during migration, searching for seeds and insects. Like a chicken, it will "double-scratch" with both feet at the same time to look for food. Gives a series of rich notes lasting 2–3 seconds, usually singing from a perch hidden in a shrub. The common name "Sparrow" comes from the Anglo-Saxon word *spearwa*, meaning "flutterer," and applies to any small bird. "Fox" refers to its rusty color. Appears in several color variations, depending on the part of the country. A winter resident of southern Arizona.

male
p. 91

female

Blue Grosbeak
Passerina caerulea

SUMMER
MIGRATION

Size: 7" (18 cm)

Female: Overall brown with darker wings and tail. Two tan wing bars. Large gray-to-silver bill.

Male: blue bird with 2 chestnut wing bars; large gray-to-silver bill; black around base of bill

Juvenile: similar to female

Nest: cup; female builds; 1–2 broods per year

Eggs: 3–6; pale blue without markings

Incubation: 11–12 days; female incubates

Fledging: 9–10 days; female and male feed the young

Migration: complete, to Mexico and Central America

Food: insects, seeds; will come to seed feeders

Compare: The female Lazuli Bunting (p. 121) and Indigo Bunting (p. 119) are similar, but they have two narrow white wing bars and are lighter color overall.

Stan's Notes: This grosbeak returns to Arizona late, by early May. A bird of semi-open habitats such as overgrown fields, riversides, woodland edges and fencerows. Visits seed feeders. Often seen twitching and spreading its tail. The first-year males show only some blue, obtaining the full complement of blue feathers in the second winter. It has expanded northward, and its overall populations have increased over the past 30–40 years.

female

male

Horned Lark
Eremophila alpestris

YEAR-ROUND

Size: 7–8" (18–20 cm)

Male: Tan to brown with black markings on the face. Black necklace and bill. Pale-yellow chin. Two tiny feather "horns" on the top of the head, sometimes hard to see. Dark tail with white outer tail feathers, seen in flight.

Female: duller than male; less noticeable "horns"

Juvenile: lacks a yellow chin and black markings; does not develop "horns" until the second year

Nest: ground; female builds; 2–3 broods per year

Eggs: 3–4; gray with brown markings

Incubation: 11–12 days; female incubates

Fledging: 9–12 days; female and male feed the young

Migration: non-migrator to partial migrator in Arizona; moves around in winter to find food

Food: seeds, insects

Compare: Western Meadowlark (p. 377) is larger and has a yellow breast and belly. Look for the black markings by the eyes and the black necklace to identify the Horned Lark.

Stan's Notes: The only true lark native to North America. A bird of open ground. Common in rural areas; often seen in large flocks. The population increased in North America over the past century as more land was cleared for farming. Male performs a fluttering courtship flight high in the air while singing a high-pitched song. Female performs a fluttering distraction display when the nest is disturbed. Starts breeding early in the year. Able to renest about a week after the brood fledges. Moves around in winter to find food. "Lark" comes from the Middle English *laverock*, or "a lark."

male

female

Arizona Woodpecker
Leuconotopicus arizonae

YEAR-ROUND

Size: 7–8" (18–20 cm)

Male: Dirty-brown back with darker wings and tail. Heavily marked chest and belly. Large white patch on side of head. Red mark on back of head.

Female: same as male but lacks the red mark and is overall lighter brown

Juvenile: chest has heavier marks, juvenile males have red spot on top of head

Nest: cavity in dead tree; male excavates; 1–2 broods per year

Eggs: 2–4; white without markings

Incubation: 12–15 days; male and female incubate

Fledging: 11–15 days; female and male feed the young

Migration: non-migrator to partial migrator in Arizona

Food: insects, acorns, berries

Compare: Hairy Woodpecker (p. 65) is larger and has a black-and-white back. Ladder-backed Woodpecker (p. 61) is similar in size and has an obvious black-and-white ladder-like pattern on back.

Stan's Notes: A native woodpecker to southeast Arizona and New Mexico. Their range extends well down into Mexico. Was once considered the same as the Strickland's Woodpecker but was split away and now considered its own species. Usually found in oak woodlands, where it is seen tapping on trees looking for insects. Feeds mainly on insects larvae but will also eat acorns. Nest activity starts in winter and by spring they are incubating eggs.

male
p. 25

female

Brown-headed Cowbird
Molothrus ater

YEAR-ROUND
SUMMER
WINTER

Size: 7½" (19 cm)

Female: Dull brown with no obvious markings. Pointed, sharp gray bill. Dark eyes.

Male: glossy black with a chocolate-brown head

Juvenile: similar to female but with dull-gray plumage and a streaked chest

Nest: no nest; lays eggs in the nests of other birds

Eggs: 5–7; white with brown markings

Incubation: 10–13 days; host birds incubate the eggs

Fledging: 10–11 days; host birds feed the young

Migration: partial to non-migrator in Arizona

Food: insects, seeds; will come to seed feeders

Compare: Female Bronzed Cowbird (p. 147) has red eyes and darker-brown wings. The female Red-winged Blackbird (p. 161) has white eyebrows and heavy streaking. European Starling (p. 27) has speckles and a shorter tail. The pointed gray bill helps to identify the female Brown-headed Cowbird.

Stan's Notes: Cowbirds are members of the blackbird family. Of approximately 750 species of parasitic birds worldwide, this is one of two parasitic birds in Arizona. Brood parasites lay their eggs in the nests of other birds, leaving the host birds to raise their young. Cowbirds are known to have laid their eggs in the nests of over 200 species of birds. While some birds reject cowbird eggs, most incubate them and raise the young, even to the exclusion of their own. Look for warblers and other birds feeding young birds twice their own size. Named "Cowbird" for its habit of following bison and cattle herds to feed on insects flushed up by the animals.

female

male
p. 29

juvenile

Bronzed Cowbird
Molothrus aeneus

YEAR-ROUND
SUMMER
MIGRATION

Size: 8" (20 cm)

Female: Overall dull brown-to-gray bird with darker brown wings and tail. A thick, pointed and slightly downward-curving gray bill. Bright-red eyes. Short tail.

Male: black plumage with glossy blue wings and tail, a thick, pointed, slightly down-curved black bill, bright-red eyes, short tail

Juvenile: similar to female, but dull-red eyes, and bill is lighter in color

Nest: no nest; lays eggs in nests of other birds

Eggs: 5–7; pale bluish green without markings

Incubation: 10–12 days; host bird incubates eggs

Fledging: 10–11 days; host birds feed young

Migration: complete migrator, to Mexico; some stay year-round in a small part of Arizona

Food: insects, seeds; comes to ground feeders

Compare: Female Brown-headed Cowbird (pg. 145) lacks red eyes and darker-brown wings.

Stan's Notes: One of two parasitic bird species in Arizona. Adults are easy to identify and differentiate from other birds by their bright-red eyes. During courtship, male throws head back, ruffles feathers and bounces up and down in front of female. Usually seen in small flocks with other species. Most are migrators, but some remain in southwestern Arizona. Known to parasitize over 70 species of birds. Female pierces host bird's eggs, which kills the young, then lays her eggs in the nest. Some birds reject cowbird eggs, but most incubate them and raise the young, even to the exclusion of their own. Like other cowbirds, this species is a member of the blackbird family.

1 year
old

Bohemian
Waxwing

Cedar Waxwing
Bombycilla cedrorum

Size: 7½" (19 cm)

Male: Sleek-looking, gray-to-brown bird. Pointed crest, bandit-like mask and light-yellow belly. Bold-yellow tip of tail. Red wing tips look like they were dipped in red wax.

Female: same as male

Juvenile: grayish with a heavily streaked breast; lacks the sleek look, black mask and red wing tips

Nest: cup; female and male construct; 1 brood per year, occasionally 2

Eggs: 4–6; pale blue with brown markings

Incubation: 10–12 days; female incubates

Fledging: 14–18 days; female and male feed the young

Migration: complete migrator; moves around to find food

Food: cedar cones, fruit, insects

Compare: Similar to its larger, less common cousin, Bohemian Waxwing (see inset). Female Northern Cardinal (p. 157) has a large red bill. Look for the red wing tips, yellow-tipped tail and black mask to identify the Cedar Waxwing.

Stan's Notes: The name is derived from its red, wax-like wing tips and preference for the small, berry-like cones of the cedar. Seen in flocks, moving around from area to area looking for berries. Feeds on insects during summer, before berries are abundant. Wanders during winter, searching for food supplies. Spends most of its time at the top of tall trees. Listen for the high pitched "sreee" whistling sound it constantly makes while perched or in flight. Obtains the mask after the first year and red wing tips after the second year. Doesn't nest in Arizona. Bohemian Waxwings visit northern Arizona in some winters.

Common Poorwill
Phalaenoptilus nuttallii

YEAR-ROUND
SUMMER

Size: 7¾" (19.5 cm)

Male: A small all-brown bird with short tail and short rounded wings. White necklace and tip of tail.

Female: same as male

Juvenile: similar to adult

Nest: no nest; female scrapes a depression in the gravel; 1–2 broods per year

Eggs: 1–2; pale white with brown markings

Incubation: 20–21 days; female and male incubate

Fledging: 20–23 days; female and male feed the young

Migration: complete migrator, to southern Arizona, Mexico, and Central and South America

Food: insects

Compare: The Lesser Nighthawk (p. 165) is very similar, but larger, with a long narrow tail and white band across each wing, as seen in flight.

Stan's Notes: Not much is known about this secretive species. It nests in open places below 8,000 feet (2,450 m) of elevation. The excellent camouflage coloring and habit of not flushing off its nest or roost make this bird hard to find and study. A nocturnal bird, usually only seen flying at dusk, flitting its wings more like a moth than a bird. Feeds on flying insects and drinks from the surface of water while in flight. Often easier to hear than to see at night. Gives a soft, low "poor-will" whistle, which accounts for the common name. Some that don't migrate have been found in a hibernation-like state (torpor).

winter

breeding

Spotted Sandpiper
Actitis macularius

SUMMER
MIGRATION
WINTER

Size: 8" (20 cm)

Male: Olive-brown back with black spots on a white chest and belly. White line over eyes. Long, dull-yellow legs. Long bill. Winter plumage lacks spots on the chest and belly.

Female: same as male

Juvenile: similar to winter plumage, with a darker bill

Nest: ground; male builds; 2 broods per year

Eggs: 3–4; brownish with brown markings

Incubation: 20–24 days; male incubates

Fledging: 17–21 days; male feeds the young

Migration: complete migrator, to southern Arizona, Mexico, Central and South America

Food: aquatic insects

Compare: Killdeer (p. 177) has 2 black neck bands. Look for the black spots on the chest and belly and the bobbing tail to help identify the breeding Spotted Sandpiper.

Stan's Notes: One of the few sandpipers in Arizona. Seen along the shorelines of large ponds, lakes and rivers. One of the few shorebirds that will dive underwater when pursued. Able to fly straight up out of the water. Holds wings in a cup-like arc in flight, rarely lifting them above a horizontal plane. Walks as if delicately balanced. When standing, constantly bobs its tail. Gives a rapid series of "weet-weet-weet" calls when frightened and flying away. Female mates with multiple males and lays eggs in up to five nests. Male does all of the nest building, incubating and childcare without any help from the female.

male
p. 335

female

Black-headed Grosbeak

Pheucticus melanocephalus

SUMMER
MIGRATION

Size:	8" (20 cm)
Female:	Appears like an overgrown sparrow. Overall brown with a lighter breast and belly. Large two-toned bill. Prominent white eyebrows. Yellow wing linings, as seen in flight.
Male:	burnt-orange chest, neck and rump, black head, tail and wings with irregular-shaped white wing patches, large bill with upper bill darker than lower
Juvenile:	similar to adult of the same sex
Nest:	cup; female builds; 1 brood per year
Eggs:	3–4; pale green or bluish, brown markings
Incubation:	11–13 days; female and male incubate
Fledging:	11–13 days; female and male feed young
Migration:	complete, to Mexico
Food:	seeds, insects, fruit; comes to seed feeders
Compare:	Female House Finch (p. 111) is smaller, has more streaking on the chest and the bill isn't as large. Look for female Grosbeak's unusual bicolored bill.

Stan's Notes: A cosmopolitan bird that nests in a wide variety of habitats. Both the male and female sing and will aggressively defend the nest against intruders. Song is very similar to American Robin's (p. 279) and Western Tanager's (p. 365), making it hard to tell them apart by song. Populations increasing in Arizona and across the U.S.

male
p. 343

female

juvenile

Northern Cardinal
Cardinalis cardinalis

Size: 8–9" (20–23 cm)

Female: Buff-brown with red tinges on the crest and wings. Black mask and a large reddish bill.

Male: red with a large crest and bill and a black mask extending from the face to the throat

Juvenile: same as female but with a blackish-gray bill

Nest: cup; female builds; 2–3 broods per year

Eggs: 3–4; bluish white with brown markings

Incubation: 12–13 days; female and male incubate

Fledging: 9–10 days; female and male feed the young

Migration: non-migrator

Food: seeds, insects, fruit; comes to seed feeders

Compare: The Cedar Waxwing (p. 149) has a small dark bill. The juvenile Northern Cardinal (bottom inset) looks like the adult female but with a dark bill. Look for the reddish bill to identify the female Northern Cardinal.

Stan's Notes: A familiar backyard bird. Seen in a variety of habitats, including parks. Usually likes thick vegetation. One of the few species in which both females and males sing. Can be heard all year. Listen for its "whata-cheer-cheer-cheer" territorial call in spring. Watch for a male feeding a female during courtship. The male also feeds the young of the first brood while the female builds a second nest. Territorial in spring, fighting its own reflection in a window or other reflective surface. Non-territorial in winter, gathering in small flocks of up to 20 birds. Makes short flights from cover to cover, often landing on the ground. *Cardinalis* denotes importance, as represented by the red priestly garments of Catholic cardinals.

157

YEAR-ROUND

Cactus Wren
Campylorhynchus brunneicapillus

Size: 8½" (22 cm)

Male: Large round-bodied wren with a chestnut-brown crown and a long tail. Many dark spots on upper breast to throat, often forming a central dark patch. Bold white eyebrows. Large, slightly downward-curving bill.

Female: same as male

Juvenile: similar to adult, shorter bill, lacks a spotty dark patch on breast

Nest: covered cup, domed or ball-shaped; female and male build; 2–3 broods per year

Eggs: 3–4; pale white to pink with brown marks

Incubation: 14–16 days; female incubates

Fledging: 19–23 days; female and male feed young

Migration: non-migrator

Food: insects, fruit, seeds; comes to seed feeders and water elements

Compare: Sage Thrasher (p. 269) is gray and lacks a down-curving bill. The Curve-billed Thrasher (p. 287) has a longer bill. Look for the Cactus Wren's prominent white eyebrows to help identify.

Stan's Notes: Our largest wren. Backyard bird with a loud "krr-krr-krr-krr-krr" or "cha-cha-cha-cha" call. Male crouches, extends wings, fans tail and growls to female during courtship. Pairs stay together all year, defending territory. Builds a large nest usually in cholla or other cactus, lining the chamber with grasses and feathers. Male builds another nest while female incubates first clutch of eggs. After the last brood fledges, roosts in nest during non-breeding season.

male
p. 35

female

Red-winged Blackbird

Agelaius phoeniceus

YEAR-ROUND

Size:	8½" (22 cm)
Female:	Heavily streaked brown body. Pointed brown bill and white eyebrows.
Male:	jet black with red-and-yellow shoulder patches (epaulets) and a pointed black bill
Juvenile:	same as female
Nest:	cup; female builds; 2–3 broods per year
Eggs:	3–4; bluish green with brown markings
Incubation:	10–12 days; female incubates
Fledging:	11–14 days; female and male feed the young
Migration:	non-migrator; will move around the state to find food in winter
Food:	seeds, insects; visits seed and suet feeders
Compare:	Female Brewer's Blackbird (p. 163) and female Yellow-headed Blackbird (p. 175) are larger. Female Brown-headed and Bronzed Cowbird (pp. 145 and 147, respectively) are smaller. All four species lack white eyebrows and heavily streaked chest of the female Red-winged Blackbird.

Stan's Notes: One of the most widespread and numerous birds in Arizona. Found around marshes, wetlands, lakes and rivers. Flocks with as many as 10,000 birds have been reported. Males arrive before females and sing to defend their territory. The male repeats his call from the top of a cattail while showing off his red-and-yellow shoulder patches. The female chooses a mate and often builds her nest over shallow water in a thick stand of cattails. The male can be aggressive when defending the nest. Feeds mostly on seeds in spring and fall, and insects throughout the summer.

male
p. 37

female

Brewer's Blackbird
Euphagus cyanocephalus

YEAR-ROUND WINTER

Size: 9" (22.5 cm)

Female: Overall grayish brown. Legs and bill nearly black. While most have dark eyes, some have bright-white or pale-yellow eyes.

Male: glossy black, shining green in direct light, head purplish, white or pale-yellow eyes

Juvenile: similar to female

Nest: cup; female builds; 1–2 broods per year

Eggs: 4–6; gray with brown markings

Incubation: 12–14 days; female incubates

Fledging: 13–14 days; female and male feed young

Migration: non-migrator to partial in Arizona; will move around to find food

Food: insects, seeds, fruit

Compare: Female Brown-headed and Bronzed Cowbird (pp. 145 and 147, respectively) are smaller and lighter in color. Female Red-winged Blackbird (p. 161) is similar in size, but it has a heavily streaked chest and prominent white eyebrows.

Stan's Notes: Common blackbird often found in association with agricultural lands and seen in open areas such as wet pastures and mountain meadows. Male and some females are easily identified by their bright, nearly white eyes. It is a common cowbird host, usually nesting in a shrub, small tree or directly on the ground. Prefers to nest in small colonies of up to 20 pairs. Gathers in large flocks with cowbirds, Red-winged Blackbirds and other blackbirds to migrate. It is expanding its range in North America.

SUMMER

Lesser Nighthawk
Chordeiles acutipennis

Size: 9" (22.5 cm)

Male: Camouflaged brown, gray and white with a white chin. Distinctive white bands across wings, seen in flight. Tiny dark bill.

Female: same as male, but tan chin and wing bands

Juvenile: similar to female, more gray than brown

Nest: no nest, lays eggs on the ground; 1 brood per year

Eggs: 2; pale white to gray with markings

Incubation: 18–20 days; female incubates

Fledging: 20–22 days; female and male feed young

Migration: complete, to Mexico, Central America and South America

Food: insects caught in air

Compare: The White-throated Swift (p. 57) is much smaller and lacks Nighthawk's white bands across the wings, as seen in flight. The Common Poorwill (p. 151) is smaller with a short tail, and it lacks the white wing bands.

Stan's Notes: This is a bird of desert scrub and cultivated regions in Arizona. Often will hunt over large parking lots or in cities where insects are attracted to the lights. In the country it flies close to the ground to hunt flying insects. Often flaps with slow, moth-like wingbeats. During the day it can be seen resting and sleeping on the tops of wooden fence posts. After mating, female lays eggs on bare sand or gravel near woodland edges. Young are fed a regurgitant of bugs that parents have caught on the wing.

YEAR-ROUND

Canyon Towhee
Melozone fusca

Size: 9" (22.5 cm)

Male: Dull brown to dark gray with a salmon-pink lower belly and base of tail. Light-tan throat. Distinctive necklace of dark spots. A central dark spot on the chest. Rusty cap. Small tan patch (lore) in front of each eye. Tail darker than rest of body. Small gray bill.

Female: same as male

Juvenile: similar to adult, but has streaking on breast and necklace is not as well defined

Nest: cup; female builds; 1 brood per year

Eggs: 3–4; pale blue or white with brown marks

Incubation: 11–13 days; female incubates

Fledging: 12–13 days; female and male feed young

Migration: non-migrator

Food: seeds, insects, fruit; visits ground feeders

Compare: Abert's Towhee (p. 169) has a dark face. The Green-tailed Towhee (pg. 323) has a brighter rusty cap and bright white throat.

Stan's Notes: Usually found in desert scrub near water in the same habitat as its close cousin, Abert's Towhee. Not a cowbird host like the Abert's. Lines its bulky nest of stems and twigs with fine plant material. Often runs across the ground with head down when disturbed to quickly get to cover of shrubs or cacti. Male droops wings and quivers while "squealing" in front of the female during courtship. Comes to seeds spread on the ground or platform feeders that offer millet and sunflower seeds. Reportedly drinks dew from vegetation. Young are fed insects. Formerly called Brown Towhee.

Abert's Towhee
Melozone aberti

Size: 9½" (24 cm)

Male: Dull brown to gray with salmon-pink lower belly and base of tail. Undertail often darker than rest of body. Dark face and eyes. Small pale-gray bill. Can have a pink wash to the upper chest.

Female: same as male

Juvenile: similar to adult, but has streaking on breast and rusty wing bars

Nest: cup; female builds; 1 brood per year

Eggs: 3–4; pale blue or white with brown marks

Incubation: 11–13 days; female incubates

Fledging: 12–13 days; female and male feed young

Migration: non-migrator

Food: seeds, small insects; visits ground feeders

Compare: The Canyon Towhee (p. 167) has a central dark spot, spotty necklace and rusty crown. Green-tailed Towhee (p. 323) has a rusty-red crown and bright white throat. Abert's is usually identified by the dark face.

Stan's Notes: Usually found in desert scrub near water. Seems to be shy and will retreat to shrubs if approached. Sings a high, harsh "teek-teek chi-chi-chi." Scratches for food on the ground. Is often associated with cowbird flocks. Some populations are declining due to Brown-headed and Bronzed Cowbird parasitism. Mates form a long-term pair bond and remain on territory year-round. Loose cup nest of stems and vines, lined with strips of bark, dried grass and animal hair. Young hatch up to several days apart (asynchronous).

Burrowing Owl
Athene cunicularia

YEAR-ROUND
SUMMER

Size: 9–10" (24 cm); up to 2' wingspan

Male: Brown owl with bold white spots and a white belly. Yellow eyes. Very long legs.

Female: same as male

Juvenile: same as adult, but belly is brown

Nest: cavity, former underground mammal den; female and male line den; 1 brood per year

Eggs: 6–11; white without markings

Incubation: 26–30 days; female incubates

Fledging: 25–28 days; female and male feed young

Migration: complete, to southern Arizona and Mexico

Food: insects, mammals, lizards, birds

Compare: Western Screech-Owl (p. 273) is slightly smaller and has ear tufts. Great Horned Owl (p. 217) is more than twice the size of Burrowing and has feather tuft "horns." Burrowing spends most of its time on the ground, unlike the tree-loving Great Horned.

Stan's Notes: An owl of fields, open backyards, golf courses and airports. Nests in large family units or in small colonies. Takes over the underground dens of mammals, occasionally widening its den by kicking dirt backward. Lines den with cow pies, horse dung, grass and feathers. Some people have had success attracting these owls to their backyards by creating artificial dens. Often seen during the day, standing or sleeping around den entrance. Male brings food to incubating female, often moving family to a new den when young are just a few weeks old. Will bob head up and down while doing deep knee bends when agitated or threatened.

in flight

juvenile

male

female

in-flight juvenile

American Kestrel
Falco sparverius

YEAR-ROUND

Size: 9–11" (23–28 cm); up to 2' wingspan

Male: Rust-brown back and tail. White breast with dark spots. Two vertical black lines on a white face. Blue-gray wings. Wide black band with a white edge on the tip of a rusty tail.

Female: similar to male but slightly larger, with rust-brown wings and dark bands on the tail

Juvenile: same as adult of the same sex

Nest: cavity; does not build a nest; 1 brood per year

Eggs: 4–5; white with brown markings

Incubation: 29–31 days; male and female incubate

Fledging: 30–31 days; female and male feed the young

Migration: non-migrator in Arizona

Food: insects, small mammals and birds, reptiles

Compare: Similar to other falcons. Look for two vertical black stripes on the Kestrel's face. No other small bird of prey has a rusty back and tail.

Stan's Notes: An unusual raptor because the sexes look different (dimorphic). Due to its small size, this falcon was once called a Sparrow Hawk. Hovers near roads, then dives for prey. Watch for it to pump its tail after landing on a perch. Perches nearly upright. Eats many grasshoppers. Adapts quickly to a wooden nest box. Can be extremely vocal, giving a loud series of high-pitched calls. Ability to see ultraviolet (UV) light helps it locate mice and other prey by their urine, which glows bright yellow in UV light.

male
p. 39

female

Yellow-headed Blackbird
Xanthocephalus xanthocephalus

SUMMER
MIGRATION
WINTER

Size: 9–11" (23–28 cm)

Female: Large brown bird with a dull-yellow head and chest. Slightly smaller than the male.

Male: black bird with a lemon-yellow head, breast and nape of neck, black mask, gray bill and white wing patches

Juvenile: similar to female

Nest: cup; female builds; 2 broods per year

Eggs: 3–5; greenish white with brown markings

Incubation: 11–13 days; female incubates

Fledging: 9–12 days; female feeds the young

Migration: complete, to southern Arizona and Mexico

Food: insects, seeds; will come to ground feeders

Compare: Female Red-winged Blackbird (p. 161) is smaller and has white eyebrows and heavy streaking. Look for the dull-yellow head to help identify the female Yellow-headed.

Stan's Notes: Found around marshes, wetlands and lakes. Nests in deep water, unlike its cousin, the Red-winged Blackbird, which prefers shallow water. Usually heard before seen. Gives a raspy, low, metallic-sounding call. The male is the only large black bird with a bright-yellow head. He gives an impressive mating display, flying with his head drooped and feet and tail pointing down while steadily beating his wings. Young keep low and out of sight for up to three weeks before they start to fly. Migrates in large flocks of as many as 200 birds, often with Red-winged Blackbirds and Brown-headed Cowbirds. Flocks of mainly males return in early April; females return later. Most colonies consist of 20–100 nests.

Killdeer
Charadrius vociferus

Size: 11" (28 cm)

Male: Upland shorebird with 2 black bands around the neck, like a necklace. Brown back and white belly. Bright reddish-orange rump, visible in flight.

Female: same as male

Juvenile: similar to adults, with a single neck band

Nest: ground; male scrapes; 2 broods per year

Eggs: 3–5; tan with brown markings

Incubation: 24–28 days; male and female incubate

Fledging: 25 days; male and female lead their young to food

Migration: non-migrator in Arizona

Food: insects, worms, snails

Compare: The Spotted Sandpiper (p. 153) is found around water but lacks the 2 neck bands of the Killdeer.

Stan's Notes: Technically classified as a shorebird but lives in dry habitats instead of the shore. Often found in vacant fields, gravel pits, driveways, wetland edges or along railroad tracks. The only shorebird that has two black neck bands. Known to fake a broken wing to draw intruders away from the nest; once the nest is safe, the parent will take flight. Nests are just a slight depression in a dry area and are often hard to see. Hatchlings look like miniature adults walking on stilts. Soon after hatching, the young follow their parents around and peck for insects. Gives a loud and distinctive "kill-deer" call. Migrates in small flocks.

male

female

YEAR-ROUND

Gilded Flicker
Colaptes chrysoides

Size: 11" (28 cm)

Male: Brown-and-black woodpecker with a large white rump patch visible only when flying. Black necklace. Speckled breast. Gray face, chin and neck with a red mustache (malar stripe) Yellow wing and tail linings, seen in flight.

Female: same as male, but lacks the red mustache

Juvenile: similar to female, but has dull-red eyes and bill is lighter in color

Nest: cavity; female and male excavate; 1 brood per year

Eggs: 5–7; white without markings

Incubation: 11–13 days; female and male incubate

Fledging: 24–26 days; female and male feed young

Migration: non-migrator

Food: insects

Compare: Very similar to Northern Flicker (p. 181), which is larger and lacks the brown nape.

Stan's Notes: Often on the ground eating its favorite food—ants. Its antacid saliva neutralizes the acidic defense of ants. The male is very noisy during courtship, calling, drumming and flashing its yellow wing and tail linings while facing its mate. Hybridizes with the red-shafted variety of Northern Flicker (p. 181) where ranges overlap. Look for the bright-yellow wing linings and the white rump to help identify the Gilded. Gives a loud "wacka-wacka" call identical to Northern Flickers, and a piercing "keew." Frequently usurped from nest cavity by starlings, sparrows and squirrels. Small owls and American Kestrels often use the large cavity in the years after the flicker has left.

male

red-shafted female

yellow-shafted male

yellow-shafted female

YEAR-ROUND
WINTER

Northern Flicker
Colaptes auratus

Size: 12" (30 cm)

Male: Brown and black with a red mustache and black necklace. Speckled chest. Gray head with a brown cap. Large white rump patch, seen only when flying.

Female: same as male but without a red mustache

Juvenile: same as adult of the same sex

Nest: cavity; female and male excavate; 1 brood per year

Eggs: 5–8; white without markings

Incubation: 11–14 days; female and male incubate

Fledging: 25–28 days; female and male feed the young

Migration: partial migrator to non-migrator in Arizona; moves around in winter

Food: insects (especially ants and beetles); comes to suet feeders

Compare: Gilded Flicker (p. 179) is smaller and has a brown nape. Gila Woodpecker (p. 67) has fine black-and-white barring on back.

Stan's Notes: This is the only woodpecker to regularly feed on the ground. Prefers ants and beetles and produces an antacid saliva that neutralizes the acidic defense of ants. Can be attracted to your yard with a nest box stuffed with sawdust. Yellow-shafted variety has golden-yellow wing linings and tails. Male yellow-shafteds have black mustaches; male red-shafteds have red mustaches. Hybrids between varieties occur in the Great Plains, where ranges overlap. The map shown here reflects the combined range. Often reuses an old nest. Undulates deeply during flight, flashing yellow under its wings and tail and calling "wacka-wacka" loudly. Populations swell in winter with northern migrants.

Mourning Dove
Zenaida macroura

YEAR-ROUND

Size:	12" (30 cm)
Male:	Smooth and fawn-colored. Gray patch on the head. Iridescent pink and greenish blue on the neck. Black spot behind and below the eyes. Black spots on the wings and tail. Pointed, wedged tail; white edges seen in flight.
Female:	similar to male, but lacks the pink-and-green iridescent neck feathers
Juvenile:	spotted and streaked plumage
Nest:	platform; female and male build; 2 broods per year
Eggs:	2; white without markings
Incubation:	13–14 days; male incubates during the day, female incubates at night
Fledging:	12–14 days; female and male feed the young
Migration:	non-migrator to partial migrator; will move around to find food
Food:	seeds; will visit seed and ground feeders
Compare:	Rock Pigeon (p. 295) is larger and has a wide range of color combinations. Eurasian Collared-Dove (p. 293) has a black collar on the nape of its neck.

Stan's Notes: Name comes from its mournful cooing. A ground feeder, bobbing its head as it walks. One of the few birds to drink without lifting its head, like the Rock Pigeon (p. 295). The parents feed the young (squab) a regurgitated liquid called crop-milk for their first few days of life. Platform nest is flimsy and often falls apart in storms. During takeoff and in flight, wind rushes through the bird's wing feathers, creating a characteristic whistling sound.

winter

breeding

Pied-billed Grebe
Podilymbus podiceps

YEAR-ROUND
WINTER

Size: 12–14" (30–36 cm)

Male: Small and brown with a black chin and fluffy white patch beneath the tail. Black ring around a thick, chicken-like, ivory bill. Winter bill is brown and unmarked.

Female: same as male

Juvenile: paler than adults, with white spots and a gray chest, belly and bill

Nest: floating platform; female and male build; 1 brood per year

Eggs: 5–7; bluish white without markings

Incubation: 22–24 days; female and male incubate

Fledging: 45–60 days; female and male feed the young

Migration: complete, to southwestern states, Mexico, Central America; non-migrator in Arizona

Food: crayfish, aquatic insects, fish

Compare: Look for a puffy white patch under the tail and thick, chicken-like bill to help identify.

Stan's Notes: A common resident water bird, often seen diving for food. When disturbed, it slowly sinks like a submarine, quickly compressing its feathers, forcing the air out. Was called Hell-diver due to the length of time it can stay submerged. Able to surface far from where it went under. Well suited to life on water, with short wings, lobed toes, and legs set close to the rear of its body. Swims easily but moves awkwardly on land. Very sensitive to pollution. Builds nest on a floating mat in water. "Grebe" may originate from the Breton word *krib*, meaning "crest," referring to the crested head plumes of many grebes, especially during breeding season.

male
p. 45

female

Great-tailed Grackle
Quiscalus mexicanus

YEAR-ROUND

Size: 15" (38 cm), female
18" (45 cm), male

Female: An overall brown bird with a gray-to-brown belly. Light-brown-to-white eyes, eyebrows, throat and upper portion of chest.

Male: all-black bird with iridescent purple sheen on head and back, exceptionally long tail, bright-yellow eyes

Juvenile: similar to female

Nest: cup; female builds; 1–2 broods per year

Eggs: 3–5; greenish blue with brown markings

Incubation: 12–14 days; female incubates

Fledging: 21–23 days; female feeds young

Migration: non-migrator to partial in Arizona; moves around to find food

Food: insects, fruit, seeds; comes to seed feeders

Compare: Female Brewer's Blackbird (p. 163) is much smaller and has a darker-brown chest. Female Brown-headed Cowbird (p. 145) is much smaller that Great-tailed. Look for Great-tailed Grackle's distinct light-brown eyebrows.

Stan's Notes: This is our largest grackle. It was once considered a subspecies of the Boat-tailed Grackle, which occurs in Florida and along the East and Gulf Coasts. Prefers to nest near water in an open habitat. A colony nester. Males do not participate in nest building, incubation or raising young. Males rarely fight; females squabble over nest sites and materials. Several females mate with one male. They are expanding northward, moving into northern states. Western populations tend to be larger than eastern ones. Song varies from population to population.

male

female

Green-winged Teal
Anas crecca

WINTER

Size: 14–15" (36–38 cm)

Male: Chestnut head with a dark-green patch outlined with white from the eyes to the nape of neck. Gray body and butter-yellow tail. Green patch on the wings (speculum), seen in flight.

Female: light-brown duck with black spots and a green speculum, small bill

Juvenile: same as female

Nest: ground; female builds; 1 brood per year

Eggs: 8–10; cream-white without markings

Incubation: 21–23 days; female incubates

Fledging: 32–34 days; female teaches the young to feed

Migration: complete to southwestern states and Mexico.

Food: aquatic plants and insects

Compare: Female Cinnamon Teal (p. 191) is similar to female Green-winged, but it has a dark line through the eyes and a larger bill.

Stan's Notes: One of the smallest dabbling ducks. Tips forward in water to feed off the bottom of shallow ponds. This behavior makes it vulnerable to ingesting spent lead shot, which can cause death. It walks well on land and will also feed in flooded fields and woodlands. Known for its fast and agile flight. Groups wheel and spin through the air in tight formation. The green wing patches are most obvious during flight.

Cinnamon Teal
Anas cyanoptera

YEAR-ROUND
SUMMER
WINTER

Size: 16" (40 cm)

Male: Deep cinnamon head, neck and belly. Light-brown back. Dark-gray bill. Deep-red eyes. Non-breeding male is overall brown with a red tinge.

Female: overall brown with a pale-brown head, long shovel-like bill, green patch on wings

Juvenile: similar to female

Nest: ground; female builds; 1 brood per year

Eggs: 7–12; pinkish white without markings

Incubation: 21–25 days; female incubates

Fledging: 40–50 days; female teaches young to feed

Migration: partial migrator to complete, to southern Arizona, California coast and Mexico; non-migrator in parts of Arizona

Food: aquatic plants and insects, seeds

Compare: Male Northern Shoveler (p. 331) also has cinnamon sides, but it is larger and has a green head and very large spoon-shaped bill. Female Green-winged Teal (p. 189) is similar to the Female Cinnamon Teal, but the Green-winged is smaller and has a dark line through its eyes and a green speculum.

Stan's Notes: The male is one of the most stunningly beautiful ducks. When threatened, the female feigns a wing injury to lure the predator away from her young. Prefers to nest along alkaline marshes and shallow lakes, within 75 yards (68 m) of the water. Mallards and other ducks often lay eggs in teal nests, resulting in many nests with over 15 eggs.

female

male p. 73

WINTER

Lesser Scaup
Aythya affinis

Size: 16–17" (40–43 cm)

Female: Overall brown duck with a dull-white patch at the base of a light-gray bill. Yellow eyes.

Male: white and gray; the chest and head appear nearly black but the head looks purple with green highlights in direct sun; yellow eyes

Juvenile: same as female

Nest: ground; female builds; 1 brood per year

Eggs: 8–14; olive-buff without markings

Incubation: 22–28 days; female incubates

Fledging: 45–50 days; female teaches young to feed

Migration: complete, to southwestern states, Mexico, Central America and northern South America

Food: aquatic plants and insects

Compare: Female Ring-necked Duck (p. 195) is a similar size but has a white ring around the bill. Look for the white patch at the base of the bill to help identify the female Lesser Scaup.

Stan's Notes: A common diving duck. Often seen in large flocks on lakes, ponds and sewage lagoons. Submerges itself completely to feed on the bottom of lakes (unlike dabbling ducks, which only tip forward to reach the bottom). Note the bold white stripe under the wings when in flight. The male leaves the female when she starts incubating eggs. The quantity of eggs (clutch size) increases with the female's age. This species has an interesting babysitting arrangement in which groups of young (crèches) are tended by one to three adult females. A winter resident, it doesn't breed in Arizona.

male p. 75

female

WINTER

Ring-necked Duck
Aythya collaris

Size:	16–19" (41–48 cm)
Female:	Brown with a darker-brown back and crown and lighter-brown sides. Gray face. White eye-ring with a white line behind the eye. White ring around the bill. Peaked head.
Male:	black head, chest and back; gray-to-white sides; blue bill with a bold white ring and a thinner ring at the base; peaked head
Juvenile:	similar to female
Nest:	ground; female builds; 1 brood per year
Eggs:	8–10; olive to brown without markings
Incubation:	26–27 days; female incubates
Fledging:	49–56 days; female teaches the young to feed
Migration:	complete migrator, to southwestern states, Mexico, Central America
Food:	aquatic plants and insects
Compare:	Female Lesser Scaup (p. 193) is similar in size. Look for the white ring around the bill to help identify the female Ring-necked Duck.

Stan's Notes: A common winter duck in Arizona. Often seen in larger freshwater lakes, usually in small flocks or just pairs. A diving duck, watch for it to dive underwater to forage for food. Springs up off the water to take flight. Has a distinctive tall, peaked head with a sloped forehead. Flattens its crown when diving. Male gives a quick series of grating barks and grunts. Female gives high-pitched peeps. Named "Ring-necked" for its cinnamon collar, which is nearly impossible to see in the field. Also called Ring-billed Duck due to the white ring on its bill.

male
p. 305

female

Gadwall
Mareca strepera

Size: 19" (48 cm)

Female: Mottled brown with a pronounced color change from dark-brown body to light-brown neck and head. Bright-white wing linings, seen in flight. Small white wing patch, seen when swimming. Gray bill with orange sides.

Male: plump gray duck with a brown head and distinctive black rump, white belly, bright-white wing linings, small white wing patch, chestnut-tinged wings, gray bill

Juvenile: similar to female

Nest: ground; female lines the nest with fine grass and down feathers plucked from her chest; 1 brood per year

Eggs: 8–11; white without markings

Incubation: 24–27 days; female incubates

Fledging: 48–56 days; young feed themselves

Migration: complete, to Arizona, southwestern states and Mexico

Food: aquatic insects

Compare: Female Mallard (p. 203) is similar but has a blue-and-white wing mark. Look for Gadwall's white wing patch and gray bill with orange sides.

Stan's Notes: A duck of shallow marshes. Consumes mostly plant material, dunking its head in water to feed rather than tipping forward, like other dabbling ducks. Walks well on land; feeds in fields and woodlands. Nests within 300 feet (90 m) of water. Often in pairs with other duck species. Establishes pair bond during winter.

male p. 345

female

WINTER

Redhead
Aythya americana

Size: 19" (48 cm)

Female: Soft-brown, plain-looking duck with gray-to-white wing linings. Rounded top of head. Two-toned bill, gray with a black tip.

Male: rich-red head and neck with a black chest and tail, gray sides, smoky-gray wings and back, tricolored bill with a light-blue base, white ring and black tip

Juvenile: similar to female

Nest: cup; female builds; 1 brood per year

Eggs: 9–14; pale white without markings

Incubation: 24–28 days; female and male incubate

Fledging: 56–73 days; female shows young what to eat

Migration: complete migrator, to Arizona, southwestern states, Mexico and Central America

Food: seeds, aquatic plants, insects

Compare: Female Northern Shoveler (p. 201) is similar, but it is lighter brown and has an exceptionally large, shovel-shaped bill.

Stan's Notes: A duck of permanent large bodies of water. Forages along the shoreline, feeding on seeds, aquatic plants and insects. Usually builds nest directly on the water's surface, using large mats of vegetation. Female lays up to 75 percent of its eggs in the nests of other Redheads and several other duck species. Nests primarily in the Prairie Pothole region of the northern Great Plains. Overall populations seem to be increasing at about 2–3 percent each year. Winters in Arizona wherever it can find water.

male p. 331

female

Northern Shoveler
Anas clypeata

MIGRATION
WINTER

Size: 19–21" (48–53 cm)

Female: A medium-sized brown duck speckled with black. Green patch on the wings (speculum). An extraordinarily large, spoon-shaped bill.

Male: iridescent green head, rusty sides, white chest and a large spoon-shaped bill

Juvenile: same as female

Nest: ground; female builds; 1 brood per year

Eggs: 9–12; olive without markings

Incubation: 22–25 days; female incubates

Fledging: 30–60 days; female leads the young to food

Migration: complete migrator, to Arizona, Mexico, and Central America

Food: aquatic insects, plants

Compare: Female Mallard (p. 203) is similar but lacks the Shoveler's large bill. Female Redhead (p. 199) is overall lighter brown and has a dark-gray bill with a black tip. Look for Shoveler's large spoon-shaped bill to help identify.

Stan's Notes: One of several species of shovelers. Called "Shoveler" due to the peculiar, shovel-like shape of its bill. Given the common name "Northern" because it is the only species of these ducks in North America. Seen in shallow wetlands, ponds and small lakes in flocks of 5–10 birds. Flocks fly in tight formation. Swims low in water, pointing its large bill toward the water as if it's too heavy to lift. Usually swims in tight circles while feeding. Feeds mainly by filtering tiny aquatic insects and plants from the surface of the water with its bill. Winters in Arizona wherever it can find water.

male
p. 329

female

Mallard
Anas platyrhynchos

YEAR-ROUND

Size:	19–21" (48–53 cm)
Female:	Brown duck with a blue-and-white wing mark (speculum). Orange-and-black bill.
Male:	large green head, white necklace, rust-brown or chestnut chest, gray-and-white sides, yellow bill, orange legs and feet
Juvenile:	same as female but with a yellow bill
Nest:	ground; female builds; 1 brood per year
Eggs:	7–10; greenish to whitish, unmarked
Incubation:	26–30 days; female incubates
Fledging:	42–52 days; female leads the young to food
Migration:	partial to non-migrator in Arizona
Food:	seeds, plants, aquatic insects; will come to ground feeders offering corn
Compare:	Female Gadwall (p. 197) has a gray bill with orange sides. Female Northern Pintail (p. 205) is similar to female Mallard, but it has a gray bill. Female Northern Shoveler (p. 201) has a spoon-shaped bill.

Stan's Notes: A familiar dabbling duck of lakes and ponds. Also found in rivers, streams and some backyards. Tips forward to feed on vegetation on the bottom of shallow water. The name "Mallard" comes from the Latin word *masculus,* meaning "male," referring to the male's habit of taking no part in raising the young. Female and male have white underwings and white tails, but only the male has black central tail feathers that curl upward. The female gives a classic quack.

Northern Pintail
Anas acuta

Size: 20" (52 cm), female
25" (63 cm), male

Male: A slender, elegant duck with a brown head, white neck and gray body. Gray bill. Extremely long and narrow black tail. Non-breeding male has a pale-brown head that lacks the clear demarcation between the brown head and white neck. Lacks long tail feathers.

Female: mottled brown body with a paler head and neck, long tail, gray bill

Juvenile: similar to female

Nest: ground; female builds; 1 brood per year

Eggs: 6–9; olive-green without markings

Incubation: 22–25 days; female incubates

Fledging: 36–50 days; female teaches young to feed

Migration: complete migrator, to Arizona, southwestern states and Mexico

Food: aquatic plants and insects, seeds

Compare: The male Northern Pintail has a distinctive brown head and white neck and unique long tail feathers. Female Mallard (p. 203) is similar to female Pintail, but Mallard has an orange bill with black spots.

Stan's Notes: A common dabbling duck of marshes in Arizona in the winter. About 90 percent of its diet is aquatic plants, except when females feed heavily on aquatic insects prior to nesting, presumably to gain extra nutrients for egg production. Male holds tail upright from the water's surface. No other North American duck has such a long tail.

male
p. 303

female

soaring

Northern Harrier
Circus hudsonius

YEAR-ROUND
WINTER

Size: 18–22" (45–56 cm); up to 4' wingspan

Female: Slender, low-flying hawk with a dark-brown back and brown streaking on the chest and belly. Large white rump patch. Thin black tail bands and black wing tips. Yellow eyes.

Male: silver-gray with a large white rump patch and white belly, black wing tips, yellow eyes, faint, thin bands across the tail

Juvenile: similar to female, with an orange breast

Nest: ground; female and male construct; 1 brood per year

Eggs: 4–8; bluish white without markings

Incubation: 31–32 days; female incubates

Fledging: 30–35 days; male and female feed the young

Migration: partial to complete, to Arizona, southwestern states, Mexico and Central America

Food: mice, snakes, insects, small birds

Compare: Slimmer than the Red-tailed Hawk (p. 211). Look for the characteristic low gliding and the black tail bands to identify the female Harrier.

Stan's Notes: One of the easiest of hawks to identify. Glides just above the ground, following the contours of the land while searching for prey. Holds its wings just above horizontal, tilting back and forth in the wind, similar to the Turkey Vulture. Formerly called Marsh Hawk due to its habit of hunting over marshes. Feeds and nests on the ground. Will also preen and rest on the ground. Unlike other hawks, mainly uses its hearing to find prey, followed by its sight. At any age, it has a distinctive owl-like face disk.

soaring light morph

intermediate morph

light morph

dark morph

soaring dark morph

Swainson's Hawk
Buteo swainsoni

SUMMER MIGRATION

Size: 19–22" (48–56 cm); up to 4¾' wingspan

Male: Highly variable plumage with three easily distinguishable color morphs. Light morph is brown and has a white belly, warm rusty chest and white face. Intermediate has a dark chest, rusty belly and white at the base of bill. Dark morph is nearly all dark brown with a rusty color low on the belly.

Female: same as male

Juvenile: similar to adult

Nest: platform; female and male construct; 1 brood per year

Eggs: 2–4; bluish or white with some brown marks

Incubation: 28–35 days; female and male incubate

Fledging: 28–30 days; female and male feed young

Migration: complete, to Central and South America

Food: small mammals, insects, snakes, birds

Compare: Slimmer than Red-tailed Hawk (p. 211), which has a white chest and brown belly band. Swainson's Hawk has longer, more pointed wings and a longer tail. Ferruginous Hawk (p. 215) has a light trailing edge of wings.

Stan's Notes: A slender open country hawk that hunts mammals, insects, snakes and birds when soaring (kiting) or perching. Often flies with slightly upturned wings in a teetering, vulture-like flight. The light morph is the most common, but the intermediate and dark are also common. Even minor nest disturbance can cause nest failure. Often gathers in large flocks to migrate.

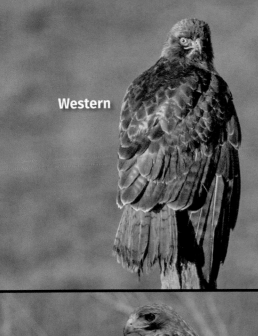

Western

soaring

Eastern

juvenile
soaring

soaring

juvenile

YEAR-ROUND

Red-tailed Hawk
Buteo jamaicensis

Size: 19–23" (48–63 cm); up to 4½' wingspan

Male: Variety of colorations, from chocolate brown to nearly all white. Often brown with a white breast and brown belly band. Rust-red tail. Underside of wing is white with a small dark patch on the leading edge near the shoulder.

Female: same as male but slightly larger

Juvenile: similar to adults, with a speckled breast and light eyes; lacks a red tail

Nest: platform; male and female build; 1 brood per year

Eggs: 2–3; white without markings or sometimes marked with brown

Incubation: 30–35 days; female and male incubate

Fledging: 45–46 days; male and female feed the young

Migration: non-migrator; moves around to find food

Food: small and medium-sized animals, large birds, snakes, fish, insects, bats, carrion

Compare: Harris's Hawk (p. 213) lacks the white breast. Swainson's Hawk (p. 209) is slimmer with longer, more pointed wings and longer tail.

Stan's Notes: Common in open country and cities. Seen perching on fences, freeway lampposts and trees. Look for it circling above open fields and roadsides, searching for prey. Gives a high-pitched scream that trails off. Often builds a large stick nest in large trees along roads. Lines nest with finer material, like evergreen needles. Returns to the same nest site each year. The red tail develops in the second year and is best seen from above. Western variety has a brown chin, while Eastern has a white chin. Map reflects the combined range.

soaring

juvenile

YEAR-ROUND

Harris's Hawk
Parabuteo unicinctus

Size: 20–22" (50 cm); up to 4' wingspan

Male: Overall dark brown hawk with rusty brown shoulders, wing linings and legs. Yellow base of bill. Bright white rump. Black tail with a bright white tip. Rusty wing linings, seen in flight. Long yellow legs. Yellow feet.

Female: same as male, but slightly larger

Juvenile: overall lighter brown with white streaks on breast, brown tail

Nest: platform; female and male build; 1–2 broods per year

Eggs: 3–4; pale white with some brown markings

Incubation: 33–36 days; female and male incubate

Fledging: 43–49 days; female and male feed young

Migration: non-migrator

Food: small mammals, snakes, birds, large insects

Compare: Red-tailed Hawk (p. 211) has a white breast and lacks rusty markings on wings. Look for Harris's white rump and white-tipped black tail.

Stan's Notes: Usually in semiarid woodlands near water. Common in city parks and suburban yards. Unlike most raptors, it hunts in small groups, usually family members. Cooperative hunting is more successful than solo hunting and enables capture of larger prey, such as jackrabbits. Nest duties often shared between females and males and sometimes by other family members. Young hatch up to a few days apart (asynchronous), leading to young developing at different times. Parents feed the young for up to six months. Produces a second brood in years with abundant food.

soaring

soaring
juvenile

juvenile

Ferruginous Hawk
Buteo regalis

**YEAR-ROUND
WINTER**

Size: 22–26" (56–66 cm); up to 4' wingspan

Male: Pale-brown head, gray cheeks, and reddish back. White chin, chest and belly. Rust flanks extend down feathered legs. Bright-white undersides of wings. Light-rust wing linings. Tail white below, rust-tinged on top. Large, strong yellow feet. Red eyes. Dark eye line.

Female: same as male, but noticeably larger

Juvenile: brown head, nape, back and wings with a white chin, chest and belly

Nest: massive platform, low in a tree, sometimes on the ground; female and male construct; 1 brood per year

Eggs: 2–4; bluish or white, can have brown marks

Incubation: 28–33 days; female and male incubate

Fledging: 44–48 days; female and male feed young

Migration: non-migrator to partial in Arizona

Food: larger mammals, snakes, insects, birds

Compare: Swainson's Hawk (p. 209) is smaller and has a dark trailing edge of wings. Red-tailed Hawk (p. 211) has a brown belly band and lacks rusty flanks and legs.

Stan's Notes: The largest hawk species. Found in western prairies. Common name means "iron-like," referring to the rusty color. Male and female perform aerial courtships, soaring with wings held above their backs, male diving at female, grabbing each other with large, powerful feet. Often hunts larger mammals, such as jackrabbits. Often stands on the ground. Seen year-round in northern Arizona. Northern Ferruginous Hawks come into Arizona in winter, increasing the population.

Great Horned Owl
Bubo virginianus

YEAR-ROUND

Size: 21–25" (53–64 cm); up to 4' wingspan

Male: Robust brown "horned" owl. Bright-yellow eyes and a V-shaped white throat resembling a necklace. Horizontal barring on the chest.

Female: same as male but slightly larger

Juvenile: similar to adults but lacks ear tufts

Nest: no nest; takes over the nest of a crow, hawk or Great Blue Heron or uses a partial cavity, stump or broken tree; 1 brood per year

Eggs: 2–3; white without markings

Incubation: 26–30 days; female incubates

Fledging: 30–35 days; male and female feed the young

Migration: non-migrator

Food: mammals, birds (ducks), snakes, insects

Compare: Burrowing Owl (p. 171) is much smaller, has long legs and lacks the Great Horned's feather tuft "horns." Over twice the size of its cousin, Western Screech-Owl (p. 273).

Stan's Notes: The largest owl in the state. One of the earliest nesting birds in Arizona, laying eggs in January and February. Able to hunt in complete darkness due to its excellent hearing. The "horns," or "ears," are tufts of feathers and have nothing to do with hearing. Cannot turn its head all the way around. Wing feathers are ragged on the ends, resulting in silent flight. Eyelids close from the top down, like humans. Fearless, it is one of the few animals that will kill skunks and porcupines. Given that, it is also called the Flying Tiger. Call sounds like "hoo-hoo-hoo-hoooo."

displaying

YEAR-ROUND

Greater Roadrunner
Geococcyx californianus

Size: 23" (58 cm)

Male: Overall brown with white streaking. Long, pointed brown bill. Extremely long tail. Blue patch just behind eyes. Short round wings are darker brown than body. Long gray legs with large feet. Has a conspicuous crest that can be raised and lowered.

Female: same as male

Juvenile: similar to adult

Nest: platform, low in a tree, shrub or cactus; the female and male build; 1–2 broods per year

Eggs: 4–6; white without markings

Incubation: 18–20 days; male and female incubate

Fledging: 16–18 days; male and female feed young

Migration: non-migrator

Food: insects, reptiles, small mammals and birds

Compare: This uniquely shaped ground dweller has an extremely long tail, a prominent crest, and is hard to confuse with other birds.

Stan's Notes: Ground dweller with a very long tail and prominent crest when raised. Cuckoo family member known to run quickly across the ground to catch prey. A formidable predator, able to run up to 15 miles (24 km) per hour. Flies short distances, usually in a low glide after a running takeoff. Raises its tail high, lowers it slowly. A slow, descending, low-pitched "coo-coo-coo-coo." Male does most incubating and feeding of young. Performs a distraction display to protect the nest. Young can catch prey four weeks after leaving the nest.

soaring

juvenile

juvenile

Golden Eagle
Aquila chrysaetos

Size: 30–40" (76–102 cm); up to 7¼' wingspan

Male: Uniform dark brown with a golden-yellow head and nape of neck. Yellow around base of bill. Yellow feet.

Female: same as male

Juvenile: similar to adult, with white "wrist" patches and a white base of tail

Nest: platform, on a cliff; female and male build; 1 brood per year

Eggs: 1–2; white with brown markings

Incubation: 43–45 days; female and male incubate

Fledging: 63–75 days; female and male feed young

Migration: non-migrator to partial migrator; moves around to find food in winter

Food: mammals, birds, reptiles, insects

Compare: The Bald Eagle (p. 81) adult is similar, but it has a white head and white tail. Bald Eagle juvenile is often confused with the Golden Eagle juvenile; both are large dark birds with white markings.

Stan's Notes: A large, powerful raptor that has no trouble taking larger prey such as jackrabbits. Hunts by perching or soaring and watching for movement. Inhabits mountainous terrain, requiring large territories to provide a sufficient supply of food. Long-term pair bond, renewing its bond late in winter with spectacular high-flying courtship displays. Usually nests on cliff faces; rarely nests in trees. Uses a well-established nest that's been used for generations. Will add items to the nest such as antlers, bones and barbed wire.

displaying male

non-displaying

female

Wild Turkey
Meleagris gallopavo

YEAR-ROUND

Size: 36–48" (91–122 cm)

Male: Large brown-and-bronze bird with a naked blue-and-red head. Long, straight, black beard in the center of the chest. Tail spreads open like a fan. Spurs on legs.

Female: thinner and less striking than the male; often lacks a breast beard

Juvenile: same as adult of the same sex

Nest: ground; female builds; 1 brood per year

Eggs: 10–12; buff-white with dull-brown markings

Incubation: 27–28 days; female incubates

Fledging: 6–10 days; female leads the young to food

Migration: non-migrator; moves around to find food

Food: insects, seeds, fruit

Compare: This bird is quite distinctive and unlikely to be confused with others.

Stan's Notes: The largest game bird in Arizona, and the species from which the domestic turkey was bred. A strong flier that can approach 60 miles (97 km) per hour. Can fly straight up, then away. Eyesight is three times better than ours. Hearing is also excellent; can hear competing males up to a mile away. Male has a "harem" of up to 20 females. Female scrapes out a shallow depression for nesting and pads it with soft leaves. Males are known as toms, females are hens, and young are poults. Roosts in trees at night.

non-breeding male

breeding male

YEAR-ROUND

Black-tailed Gnatcatcher
Polioptila melanura

Size: 4" (10 cm)

Male: Overall gray bird with a black cap and bold white ring around eyes. Light-gray throat, breast and belly. Long black tail with white edges. Non-breeding lacks the black cap.

Female: similar to non-breeding male

Juvenile: similar to female

Nest: cup; female and male construct; 1–2 broods per year

Eggs: 3–5; pale blue with brown markings

Incubation: 11–14 days; female and male incubate

Fledging: 9–15 days; female and male feed young

Migration: non-migrator

Food: insects, occasionally seeds

Compare: Mountain Chickadee (p. 243) shares the breeding male Gnatcatcher's black cap, but the Chickadee has a black chin. The White-breasted Nuthatch (p. 249) is larger and has a white face.

Stan's Notes: A small, fast-moving bird. Usually seen flitting about in trees and shrubs, searching for insects. Snaps up insects in flight or gleans them off leaves. Often lands on a branch with tail cocked upward. Flicks tail up and down and from side to side. Frequently found in mesquite, creosote bush and other desert habitat. Builds nest with plant material and glues it together with spider webs in a fork of a small shrub. Pairs often remain together all year long.

Ruby-crowned Kinglet
Regulus calendula

YEAR-ROUND
WINTER

Size: 4" (10 cm)

Male: Small, teardrop-shaped green-to-gray bird. Two white wing bars and a white eye-ring. Hidden ruby crown.

Female: same as male, but lacks a ruby crown

Juvenile: same as female

Nest: pendulous; female builds; 1 brood per year

Eggs: 4–5; white with brown markings

Incubation: 11–12 days; female incubates

Fledging: 11–12 days; female and male feed the young

Migration: complete, to Arizona, southwestern states and Mexico; non-migrator in northern Arizona

Food: insects, berries

Compare: The female American Goldfinch (p. 357) shares the drab olive plumage and unmarked chest, but it is larger. Look for the white eye-ring to identify the Ruby-crowned Kinglet.

Stan's Notes: This is one of the smaller birds in the state. Most commonly seen during the spring and autumn migrations. Look for it flitting around thick shrubs low to the ground. It takes a quick eye to see the ruby crown, which the male flashes when he is excited. The female weaves an unusually intricate nest and fastens colorful lichens and mosses to the exterior with spiderwebs. Often builds the nest high in a mature tree, where it hangs from a branch that has overlapping leaves. Sings a distinctive song that starts out soft and ends loud and on a higher note. "Kinglet" originates from the word *king*, referring to the male's red crown, and the diminutive suffix *let*, meaning "small."

male

female

Golden-crowned Kinglet
Regulus satrapa

YEAR-ROUND
WINTER

Size: 4" (10 cm)

Male: Tiny, plump green-to-gray bird. Distinctive yellow-and-orange patch with a black border on the crown (top inset). White eyebrow mark. 2 white wing bars.

Female: same as male, but has a yellow crown with a black border, lacks any orange (bottom inset)

Juvenile: same as adults, but lacks gold on crown

Nest: pendulous; female builds; 1–2 broods per year

Eggs: 5–9; white or creamy with brown markings

Incubation: 14–15 days; female incubates

Fledging: 14–19 days; female and male feed the young

Migration: non-migrator to partial, moves around to find food in winter

Food: insects, fruit, tree sap

Compare: Similar to the Ruby-crowned Kinglet (p. 227), but the Golden-crowned has an obvious crown. Female American Goldfinch (p. 357) is larger and has an all-black forehead.

Stan's Notes: Often seen in flocks with chickadees, nuthatches, woodpeckers and Ruby-crowned Kinglets. Flicks its wings when moving around. Constructs an unusual hanging nest, often with moss, lichens and spiderwebs, and lines it with bark and feathers. Can have so many eggs in its small nest that eggs are in two layers. Drinks tree sap and feeds by gleaning insects from trees. Can be very tame and approachable but constantly on the move.

Lucy's Warbler

Oreothlypis luciae

Size: 4" (10 cm)

Male: Small gray warbler with rusty-orange crown and rump. Light-tan breast and belly. Pale-white stripe through dark eyes. Darker-gray tail. Small dark bill.

Female: same as male, but has a less rusty crown

Juvenile: similar to female, lacks the rusty crown, has a pale-orange rump

Nest: cavity; female and male line an old wood-pecker hole; 1–2 broods per year

Eggs: 4–5; white with brown markings

Incubation: 10–12 days; female and male incubate

Fledging: 10–13 days; female and male feed young

Migration: complete, to Mexico and Central America

Food: insects

Compare: One of the few gray warblers. Orange-crowned Warbler (p. 361) is similar, but its crown is less noticeable than Lucy's. Look for the rusty-orange rump to help identify Lucy's Warbler.

Stan's Notes: Common warbler of mesquite scrub very near water. The only warbler species in Arizona that nests in a cavity. Female and male line an old woodpecker hole with plant material, such as strips of bark and dry leaves. Will sometimes nest behind bark that is sloughing off a dead tree. Rusty-orange crown is often hard to see, but rusty rump is obvious when the bird is in flight.

Pygmy Nuthatch
Sitta pygmaea

YEAR-ROUND

Size: 4¼" (10.5 cm)

Male: Tiny gray-blue and black bird with gray-brown crown. Creamy chest with a lighter chin. A relatively short tail, large head and long bill.

Female: same as male

Juvenile: same as adult

Nest: cavity; female and male construct; 1 brood per year

Eggs: 4–8; white with brown markings

Incubation: 14–16 days; female incubates

Fledging: 20–22 days; female and male feed young

Migration: non-migrator

Food: insects, berries, seeds; will visit seed feeders

Compare: Red-breasted Nuthatch (p. 237) is larger and has a rusty-red chest. White-breasted Nuthatch (p. 249) is larger and has a distinctive black cap and a white chest.

Stan's Notes: A nuthatch of pine forests. Unlike the White-breasted Nuthatch, the Pygmy Nuthatch requires mature pines with old or decaying wood. Usually drills its own nest cavity. While it does not migrate, it forms winter flocks with chickadees and other birds and moves around to find food. Usually feeds in the crown of a tree or at the ends of twigs and branches, where it searches for insects and seeds. This is unlike White-breasted and Red-breasted Nuthatches, which usually search trunks of trees for food.

Bushtit

Psaltriparus minimus

YEAR-ROUND

Size: 4½" (11 cm)

Male: Dull gray with a slightly brown cap. Relatively long tail. Black eyes and legs. Tiny black bill.

Female: same as male, but has pale-yellow eyes

Juvenile: similar to adults, with dark-brown eyes

Nest: pendulous; female and male construct; 1–2 broods per year

Eggs: 5–7; white without markings

Incubation: 10–12 days; female and male incubate

Fledging: 14–15 days; female and male feed young

Migration: non-migrator

Food: insects, seeds, fruit; comes to seed feeders

Compare: Mountain Chickadee (p. 243) is larger and has a black cap and white on the face. Lucy's Warbler (p. 231) is similar in size and has a rusty cap and a much longer bill.

Stan's Notes: A lively bird, often seen in extended family flocks of up to 20 individuals in open woods and low woodlands. Often seen with other species of birds, such as kinglets, wrens and chickadees. Easily picked out by its small size, long tail and the extremely short bill. Groups will roost together, huddling tightly to keep warm and save energy. Eyes are pale yellow in adult females, dark brown in juveniles and black in adult males.

Red-breasted Nuthatch
Sitta canadensis

YEAR-ROUND
WINTER

Size: 4½" (11 cm)

Male: Gray-backed bird with an obvious black eye line and black cap. Rust-red breast and belly.

Female: duller than male and has a gray cap and pale undersides

Juvenile: same as female

Nest: cavity; male and female excavate a cavity or move into a vacant hole; 1 brood per year

Eggs: 5–6; white with red-brown markings

Incubation: 11–12 days; female incubates

Fledging: 14–20 days; female and male feed the young

Migration: non-migrator to irruptive; moves around in winter in search of food

Food: insects, insect eggs, seeds; comes to seed and suet feeders

Compare: Pygmy Nuthatch (p. 233) is smaller and White-breasted Nuthatch (p. 249) is larger, and neither has the rust-red breast and black eye line of Red-breasted Nuthatch.

Stan's Notes: The nuthatch climbs down trunks of trees headfirst, searching for insects. Like a chickadee, it grabs a seed from a feeder and flies off to crack it open. It wedges the seed into a crevice and pounds it open with several sharp blows. The name "Nuthatch" comes from the Middle English moniker *nuthak*, referring to the habit of hacking seeds open. Look for it in mature conifers, where it extracts seeds from pine cones. Excavates a cavity or takes an old woodpecker hole or a natural cavity and builds a nest within. Gives a series of nasal "yank-yank-yank" calls.

male

juvenile

female

Verdin

Auriparus flaviceps

Size: 4½" (11 cm)

Male: Light gray to silvery overall. Lemon-yellow head. Rusty-red shoulder patch, frequently hidden. Short, pointed dark bill. Dark mark between bill and eyes. Dark legs and feet.

Female: duller than male

Juvenile: overall gray, lacks the yellow head, dark bill and rusty-red shoulder patch

Nest: covered cup; male builds; 1–2 broods a year

Eggs: 4–5; bluish green with brown markings

Incubation: 8–10 days; female incubates

Fledging: 19–21 days; female and male feed young

Migration: non-migrator

Food: seeds, insects, fruit, nectar; comes to nectar feeders and orange halves

Compare: Juniper Titmouse (p. 253) is larger, has a crest and lacks the yellow head. Mountain Chickadee (p. 243) has an obvious black cap, chin and eye line.

Stan's Notes: A very friendly bird that can be a regular visitor to nectar feeders and orange halves. Often hides its rusty-red shoulder marks, confusing the novice bird watcher. Most easily identified as a tiny gray bird with a yellow head. Male builds several ball-shaped, conspicuous nests of thorny twigs, interweaves them with leaves and grass and lines them with feathers and plant down. Male shows the nest possibilities to female and she selects one. After fledging, young return to nest at night, unlike most small birds, which leave and don't return for shelter. Often uses nest for several seasons.

Bridled Titmouse
Baeolophus wollweberi

YEAR-ROUND
WINTER

Size: 5" (13 cm)

Male: Overall gray with bold black-and-white markings on the head. Pointed crest. Black throat. Dark bill.

Female: same as male

Juvenile: similar to adult

Nest: cavity; female and male build or line an old woodpecker hole; 1–2 broods per year

Eggs: 4–6; white without markings

Incubation: 11–13 days; female incubates

Fledging: 12–13 days; female and male feed young

Migration: non-migrator; moves around in winter to find food

Food: insects, seeds

Compare: Juniper Titmouse (p. 253) is slightly larger and lacks the black throat and "bridle" markings on head. Mountain Chickadee (p. 243) has a similar black-and-white head pattern, but it lacks a crest. Look for a small gray bird with a crest and black throat to help identify the Bridled Titmouse.

Stan's Notes: An energetic small bird of oak and pine-oak woodlands. Closely related to the Juniper Titmouse and Mountain Chickadee. The common name comes from the head pattern, which gives the appearance of a bridle. Is able to raise and lower its crest at will. A year-round resident that forms small flocks, often with other bird species, in the non-breeding season to forage for insects. Nests in a natural cavity, using fine plant material and animal fur for a lining.

Mountain Chickadee
Poecile gambeli

YEAR-ROUND

Size: 5½" (14 cm)

Male: Gray overall with a black cap, chin and line through the eyes. White eyebrows.

Female: same as male

Juvenile: similar to adult

Nest: cavity, old woodpecker hole or excavates its own; female and male build; 1–2 broods per year

Eggs: 5–8; white without markings

Incubation: 11–14 days; female and male incubate

Fledging: 18–21 days; female and male feed the young

Migration: non-migrator; moves around to find food

Food: seeds, insects; visits seed and suet feeders

Compare: Bridled Titmouse (p. 241) and Juniper Titmouse (p. 253) have a crest and lack the black cap. Verdin (p. 239) is smaller and has a yellow head. Black-tailed Gnatcatcher (p. 225) shares the black cap during breeding season, but it has a light-gray throat.

Stan's Notes: An abundant bird in the state, but most common in coniferous forests in mountainous regions of Arizona. Prefers old-growth spruce, fir and pine forests. Feeds heavily on coniferous seeds and insects. Flocks with other birds during winter. Moves to lower elevations in winter, returning to high elevations for nesting. Excavates a nest cavity or uses an old woodpecker hole. Will use a nest box. Occasionally uses the same nest site year after year. Lines its nest with moss, hair and feathers. Female will not leave her nest if disturbed, but will hiss and flutter wings.

female
p. 117

male

pink-sided

Oregon
male

YEAR-ROUND
WINTER

Dark-eyed Junco
Junco hyemalis

Size: 5½" (14 cm)

Male: Plump, dark-eyed bird with a slate-gray-to-charcoal chest, head and back. White belly. Pink bill. White outer tail feathers appear like a white V in flight.

Female: round with brown plumage

Juvenile: similar to female, with streaking on the breast and head

Nest: cup; female and male build; 2 broods per year

Eggs: 3–5; white with reddish-brown markings

Incubation: 12–13 days; female incubates

Fledging: 10–13 days; male and female feed the young

Migration: partial to non-migrator in Arizona

Food: seeds, insects; visits ground and seed feeders

Compare: Yellow-eyed Junco (p. 247) is very similar, but it has yellow eyes and a yellow lower bill. Look for small flocks under feeders in winter.

Stan's Notes: One of the most numerous wintering birds in the state and a common year-round resident in northern Arizona. Spends winters in foothills and plains, returning to higher elevations for nesting. Females tend to migrate farther south than males. Adheres to a rigid social hierarchy, with dominant birds chasing the less dominant birds. Look for the white outer tail feathers flashing in flight. Often seen in small flocks on the ground, where it uses its feet to simultaneously "double-scratch" to expose seeds and insects. Eats many weed seeds. Nests in a wide variety of wooded habitats in April and May. Several sub-species of Dark-eyed Junco were previously considered to be separate species (see lower insets).

Yellow-eyed Junco
Junco phaeonotus

Size: 6" (15 cm)

Male: Mostly gray with rusty back and wing bars. Dark patch around bright-yellow eyes. Short bicolored bill has gray upper mandible and yellow lower mandible.

Female: same as male

Juvenile: rusty-brown plumage with dark spots and streaks throughout, all-gray head, gray eyes

Nest: cup, on the ground; female and male build; 1–2 broods per year

Eggs: 3–4; pale blue with brown markings

Incubation: 12–14 days; female incubates

Fledging: 10–12 days; female and male feed young

Migration: non-migrator to partial migrator; moves to lower elevations during winter

Food: insects, seeds; will come to seed feeders and ground feeders

Compare: The male Dark-eyed Junco (p. 245) is very similar, but it has dark eyes and lacks a yellow lower bill.

Stan's Notes: Year-round resident in southeastern parts of the state in coniferous and pine-oak forests. Often in higher elevations in the summer. Walks on the ground instead of hopping. A ground feeder, often attracted to millet or other seeds scattered about. Constructs its nest in a shallow depression on the ground under overhanging vegetation. Young are pushed out of adult territories after only 30 days. Juvenile flocks are often misidentified by beginners because their plumage and eye color is so different from their parents.

male

female

YEAR-ROUND

White-breasted Nuthatch
Sitta carolinensis

Size: 5–6" (13–15 cm)

Male: Slate gray with a white face, breast and belly. Large white patch on the rump. Black cap and nape. Bill is long and thin, slightly upturned. Chestnut undertail.

Female: similar to male, but has a gray cap and nape

Juvenile: similar to female

Nest: cavity; female and male build a nest within; 1 brood per year

Eggs: 5–7; white with brown markings

Incubation: 11–12 days; female incubates

Fledging: 13–14 days; female and male feed the young

Migration: non-migrator

Food: insects, insect eggs, seeds; comes to seed and suet feeders

Compare: Red-breasted Nuthatch (p. 237) is smaller and has a rust-red belly and distinctive black eye line. Pygmy Nuthatch (p. 233) is smaller and lacks White-breasted's black cap. The Black-tailed Gnatcatcher (p. 225) lacks a white face.

Stan's Notes: The nuthatch hops headfirst down trees, looking for insects missed by birds climbing up. Its climbing agility is due to an extra-long hind toe claw, or nail, that is nearly twice the size of its front claws. "Nuthatch," from the Middle English *nuthak*, refers to the bird's habit of wedging a seed in a crevice and hacking it open. Often seen in flocks with Brown Creepers, chickadees and Downy Woodpeckers. Mates stay together year-round, defending a small territory. Gives a characteristic "whi-whi-whi-whi" spring call during February and March. One of nearly 30 worldwide nuthatch species.

male

female

first
winter

Yellow-rumped Warbler
Setophaga coronata

Size: 5–6" (13–15 cm)

Male: Slate gray with black streaking on the chest. Yellow patches on the head, flanks and rump. White chin and belly. Two white wing bars.

Female: duller gray than the male, mixed with brown

Juvenile: first winter is similar to the adult female

Nest: cup; female builds; 2 broods per year

Eggs: 4–5; white with brown markings

Incubation: 12–13 days; female incubates

Fledging: 10–12 days; female and male feed young

Migration: non-migrator to partial migrator, to Arizona, Mexico and Central America

Food: insects, berries; visits suet feeders in spring

Compare: Male Wilson's Warbler (p. 353) has a black cap. The male Common Yellowthroat (p. 359) has a yellow chest and distinctive black mask. Male Yellow Warbler (p. 363) is all yellow with orange streaks on the breast. Look for patches of yellow on the rump, head, flanks and chin of Yellow-rumped Warbler to help identify.

Stan's Notes: A common warbler in the state, nesting in conifer and aspen forests. Flocks of hundreds are seen when northern birds join residents for the winter. Familiar call is a single robust "chip," heard mostly during migration. Sings a wonderful song in spring. In the fall, the male molts to a dull color similar to the female, but he retains his yellow patches all year. Frequently called Myrtle Warbler in eastern states and Audubon's Warbler in western states. Sometimes called Butter-butt due to the yellow patch on its rump.

YEAR-ROUND

Juniper Titmouse
Baeolophus ridgwayi

Size: 6" (15 cm)

Male: All gray with a crest. Dark eyes. Small gray bill. Upper wings may have faint brown tinge.

Female: same as male

Juvenile: similar to adult, often lighter in color, lacks a well-developed crest

Nest: cavity; female builds; 1 brood per year

Eggs: 3–6; white without markings

Incubation: 14–16 days; female and male incubate

Fledging: 16–21 days; female and male feed young

Migration: non-migrator

Food: seeds, insects, fruit

Compare: Bridled Titmouse (p. 241) has a black-and-white pattern on head. Mountain Chickadee (p. 243) is slightly smaller, has a black cap and lacks a crest. Verdin (p. 239) is smaller, has a yellow head and lacks a crest.

Stan's Notes: A very drab-looking bird usually found in open dry habitats. Can be attracted to your yard with a nest box. The female does not usually fly when approached at the nest, but will fluff up and hiss to protect her eggs. Like the chickadee, it builds a similar nest with green moss and grass and lines it with animal fur. Mated pairs often remain together throughout the season. This species was once considered the same as the Oak Titmouse (*B. inornatus*).

Black-throated Sparrow
Amphispiza bilineata

YEAR-ROUND
SUMMER

Size: 6" (15 cm)

Male: Overall smooth gray bird with bold black-and-white markings on head and face. Large black patch on the throat. Darker-gray tail with white edges.

Female: same as male

Juvenile: similar to adult, lacks the black-and-white head pattern and black throat

Nest: cup; female builds; 1–2 broods per year

Eggs: 3–4; pale blue to white without markings

Incubation: 12–14 days; female incubates

Fledging: 10–12 days; female and male feed young

Migration: partial migrator to non-migrator

Food: insects, seeds, leaf buds

Compare: White-crowned Sparrow (p. 135) shares bold black-and-white coloring on the head, but it lacks the large black throat patch. Look for a black patch on the throat of a smooth gray sparrow to identify the Black-throated.

Stan's Notes: A sparrow of desert scrub and rocky uplands. Male often perches on prominent spots in its territory and sings a short, simple, tinkling song or a high, bell-like "tee-tee-tee." Often holds off breeding until rainfall produces enough food. Female constructs a cup nest of dried grass low in a cactus and lines it with finer plant materials. Although the young are fed a diet of insects, adults will eat new green shoots of trees, shrubs and grasses along with insects and seeds. Forms small flocks in the winter of up to 20 individuals, often with other sparrow species.

female

male p. 339

Vermilion Flycatcher
Pyrocephalus rubinus

Size: 6" (15 cm)

Female: A mostly gray bird with a gray head, neck and back. Nearly white chin and chest. Pink belly to undertail. Black tail. Thin black bill.

Male: crimson-red head, crest, chin, breast and belly, black nape of neck, back, wings and tail, black line through eyes, thin black bill

Juvenile: similar to female, lacks a pink undertail

Nest: cup; female builds; 1–2 broods per year

Eggs: 2–4; white with brown markings

Incubation: 14–16 days; female and male incubate

Fledging: 14–16 days; female and male feed young

Migration: partial migrator, to southern Arizona, through-out Mexico; non-migrator in parts of Arizona

Food: insects (mainly bees)

Compare: Black Phoebe and Say's Phoebe (pp. 59 and 261) have similar body and bill shapes and share a similar habitat. Black Phoebe is black with a white belly. Say's Phoebe has a pale-orange belly.

Stan's Notes: Frequently seen in open areas with shrubs and small trees close to water. Will perch on a thin branch, pumping tail up and down while waiting for an aerial insect. Flies out to snatch it, then returns to perch. Drops to the ground for terrestrial insects. Male raises its crest, fluffs chest feathers, fans tail and sings a song during a fluttery flight to court females. Female builds a shallow nest of twigs and grasses and lines it with downy plant material. Male feeds female during incubation and brooding.

SUMMER
MIGRATION

Western Wood-Pewee
Contopus sordidulus

Size: 6¼" (15.5 cm)

Male: Overall gray with darker wings and tail. Two narrow gray wing bars. Dull-white throat. Pale-yellow or white belly. Black upper bill and dull-orange lower.

Female: same as male

Juvenile: similar to adult, lacking the two-toned bill

Nest: cup; female builds; 1 brood per year

Eggs: 2–4; pale white with brown markings

Incubation: 12–14 days; female incubates

Fledging: 14–18 days; female and male feed young

Migration: complete, to Central and South America

Food: insects

Compare: Female Vermilion Flycatcher (p. 257) is slightly smaller and has a pink lower belly. Black Phoebe (p. 59) is larger and has a black head. Say's Phoebe (p. 261) is larger and has a tawny belly.

Stan's Notes: A widespread bird in Arizona that is most common in aspen forests and near water. It requires trees with dead tops or branches from which to sing and hunt for flying insects, which compose nearly all of the diet. Often returns to the same perch after each foray. Nests throughout western North America from Alaska to Mexico. Overall populations are decreasing about 1 percent each year. Common name comes from its nasal whistle, "pee-wee."

Say's Phoebe
Sayornis saya

YEAR-ROUND
SUMMER

Size: 7½" (19 cm)

Male: Overall dark gray, darkest on head, tail and wings. Belly and undertail tawny. Black bill.

Female: same as male

Juvenile: similar to adult, but browner overall with 2 tawny wing bars and a yellow lower bill

Nest: cup; female builds; 1–2 broods per year

Eggs: 3–6; pale white with brown markings

Incubation: 12–14 days; female incubates

Fledging: 14–16 days; female and male feed young

Migration: non-migrator to partial, to Arizona, other southwestern states and Mexico

Food: insects, berries

Compare: Western Wood-Pewee (p. 259) is smaller and also lacks the tawny belly. Female Vermilion Flycatcher (p. 257) is smaller and has a pink belly.

Stan's Notes: A widespread bird in Arizona below 9,000-foot (2,750 m) elevations. Nests in cliff crevices, abandoned buildings, bridges and other vertical structures. Frequently uses the same nest a couple of times in a season, returning the following year to that same nest. Has a nearly all-insect diet. Flies out from a perch to grab an aerial insect and returns to the same perch (hawking). Also hunts insects on the ground, hovering and dropping down to catch them. Phoebes are classified as New World Flycatchers and aren't related to Old World Flycatchers. Named after Thomas Say, who is said to have first recorded this bird in Colorado. The genus, species and first part of its common name refer to Mr. Say. Common name "Phoebe" is likely an imitation of the bird's call.

American Dipper
Cinclus mexicanus

YEAR-ROUND
WINTER

Size: 7½" (19 cm)

Male: Dark gray to black overall. Head is slightly lighter in color. Short upturned tail. Dark eyes and bill.

Female: same as male

Juvenile: similar to adult, only paler with white eyelids that are most noticeable when blinking

Nest: pendulous, covered nest with the entrance near the bottom; on cliffs, behind waterfalls; female builds; 1–2 broods per year

Eggs: 3–5; white without markings

Incubation: 13–17 days; female incubates

Fledging: 18–25 days; female and male feed young

Migration: non-migrator; seeks moving open water

Food: aquatic insects, small fish, crustaceans

Compare: American Robin (p. 279) is a similar shape, but it has a red breast. The Dipper is the only songbird in the state that dives into fast-moving water.

Stan's Notes: A bird of fast, usually noisy streams that provide some kind of protected shelf on which to construct a nest. Some have had success attracting with man-made ledges. Plunges headfirst into fast-moving water, looking for just about any aquatic insect, propelling itself underwater with its wings. Frequently seen emerging with a large insect, which it smashes against rock before eating. Has the ability to fly directly into the air from underwater. Depending on snowmelt, nesting usually starts in March or April. American Dippers in elevations below 6,000 feet (1,850 m) often nest for a second time each season.

Inca Dove
Columbina inca

Size: 8" (20 cm)

Male: A small thin-bodied dove, pale gray overall. Scalloped or scaly appearance due to dark-edged feathers. Lighter gray head. Dark thin bill. Dark-red eyes. Long thin tail. White outer tail feathers and dark rusty wing linings, seen in flight.

Female: same as male

Juvenile: similar to adult, lacks a scaly pattern

Nest: platform; female and male build; 2–3 broods per year

Eggs: 2; white without markings

Incubation: 12–14 days; female and male incubate

Fledging: 14–16 days; female and male feed young

Migration: non-migrator

Food: seeds, fruit; visits seed feeders on ground

Compare: One of the smallest doves in Arizona. Scaly appearance assures correct identification.

Stan's Notes: Seen in many habitats, including cities and suburbs, mostly in arid areas with some low scrubby growth. Male bows to female with tail fanned to show white sides. Outer wing feathers produce a buzzing sound in flight. Groups of up to 50 birds gather in summer and winter to find food. Roosts in large groups, sitting side by side or sometimes one on another. Huddles in "pyramids," sometimes stacked two or three individuals high. Constructs a loose platform nest of twigs, grass and leaves. Nest is sometimes built on the ground, low in a tree or shrub or in a hanging flower basket. Will also reuse the nest of larger doves, such as Mourning Doves.

male
p. 31

female

Phainopepla
Phainopepla nitens

YEAR-ROUND
SUMMER
WINTER

Size: 8" (20 cm)

Female: Slim, long, mostly gray bird with a ragged crest and deep-red eyes. Whitish wing bars.

Male: slim, long, glossy black bird with a ragged crest and deep-red eyes, wing patches near tips of wings are white, obvious in flight

Juvenile: similar to female

Nest: cup; female and male construct; 1–2 broods per year

Eggs: 2–4; gray with brown markings

Incubation: 12–14 days; female and male incubate

Fledging: 18–20 days; female and male feed young

Migration: complete, to southern Arizona and California

Food: fruit (usually mistletoe), insects; will come to water elements or water drips in yards

Compare: Clark's Nutcracker (p. 291) is similar, but lacks a crest.

Stan's Notes: Seen in desert scrub with water and mistletoe nearby. Gives a low, liquid "kweer" song, but will also mimic other species. In winter, individuals defend food supply, such as a single tree with abundant mistletoe berries. Probably responsible for the dispersal of mistletoe plants far and wide. Male will fly up to a height of 300 feet (90 m), circling and zigzagging to court female. Builds nest of twigs and plant fibers and binds it with spider webs in the crotch of a mistletoe cluster. Lines nest with hair or soft plant fibers. May be the only species to nest in two regions in the same nesting season. Nests in dry desert habitat in early spring, and when it gets hot, moves to a higher area with an abundant water supply to nest again.

Sage Thrasher
Oreoscoptes montanus

SUMMER
MIGRATION
WINTER

Size: 8½" (22 cm)

Male: Light gray overall with a heavily streaked white chest. Distinctive white chin. Yellow-orange eyes. Darker gray tail with white tip.

Female: same as male

Juvenile: duller version of adult

Nest: cup; the female and male build; 1–2 broods per year

Eggs: 3–5; blue with brown markings

Incubation: 13–17 days; female and male incubate

Fledging: 11–14 days; female and male feed young

Migration: complete, to Arizona, Mexico, Central America

Food: insects, fruit

Compare: The Curve-billed Thrasher (p. 287) lacks obvious streaks on the chest and has a long downward-curving bill. Cactus Wren (p. 159) has bold white eyebrows and a down-curved bill. Northern Mockingbird (p. 281) has white wing patches, as seen in flight.

Stan's Notes: More common in the sagebrush regions, which are known for unique birdlife. Males are often seen and heard as they sing from the tops of shrubs. Will construct a large and bulky nest at the base of or beneath dense cover in an attempt to keep the nest shaded. Sometimes constructs a twig platform over nest if existing cover doesn't provide enough shade. Old nests are sometimes used by Gambel's Quails. Returns in to nesting grounds in April and nests in May. Populations increasing in Arizona over the past few decades.

Townsend's Solitaire
Myadestes townsendi

YEAR-ROUND
WINTER

Size: 8½" (22 cm)

Male: All-gray robin look-alike. Prominent white ring around each eye. Wings slightly darker than the body. Long tail. Short dark bill. Dark legs.

Female: same as male

Juvenile: darker gray with a tan, scaly appearance

Nest: cup; female builds; 1–2 broods per year

Eggs: 3–5; blue, green, gray or white with brown markings

Incubation: 12–14 days; female incubates

Fledging: 10–14 days; female and male feed young

Migration: partial to non-migrator, to southwestern states and Mexico; known to migrate to eastern states

Food: insects, fruit

Compare: American Robin (p. 279) has a red breast. The Northern Mockingbird (p. 281) lacks the white eye-ring. Clark's Nutcracker (p. 291) has black wings.

Stan's Notes: A summer resident of coniferous mountain forests, moving lower in winter. "Hawks" for insects, perching in trees and darting out to capture them. Eats berries in winter when insects are not available and actively defends a good berry source from other birds. Builds nest on ground sheltered by rocks or an overhang, or sometimes low in a tree or shrub. Song is a series of clear flute-like whistles without a distinct pattern. Shows white outer tail feathers and light-tan patches on wings when in flight.

gray morph

brown morph

Western Screech-Owl

Megascops kennicottii

YEAR-ROUND

Size: 8–9" (20–23 cm); up to 1¾' wingspan

Male: A small, overall gray owl with bright-yellow eyes. Two short ear tufts. A short tail. Some birds are brownish.

Female: same as male

Juvenile: similar to adult of the same morph and lacks ear tufts

Nest: cavity, old woodpecker hole; 1 brood per year

Eggs: 2–6; white without markings

Incubation: 21–30 days; female incubates

Fledging: 25–30 days; male and female feed the young

Migration: non-migrator

Food: large insects, small mammals, birds

Compare: Burrowing Owl (p. 171) is slightly larger and lacks ear tufts. Western Screech-Owl is hard to confuse with its considerably larger cousin, Great Horned Owl (p. 217).

Stan's Notes: This is the most common small owl throughout Arizona. An owl of suburban woodlands and backyards. Requires trees that are at least a foot in diameter for nesting and roosting, so it usually is found in towns or in trees that have been preserved. A secondary cavity nester, which means it nests in tree cavities created by other birds. Usually not found in elevations above 4,000 feet (1,200 m). Densities in areas with lower elevations are about 1 bird per square mile (2.5 sq. km). Most screech-owls are gray; some are brown (see inset).

Loggerhead Shrike
Lanius ludovicianus

YEAR-ROUND

Size: 9" (22.5 cm)

Male: Gray head and back and a white chin, breast and belly. Black wings, tail, legs and feet. Black mask across the eyes and a black bill with a hooked tip. White wing patches, seen in flight.

Female: same as male

Juvenile: dull version of adult

Nest: cup; male and female construct; 1–2 broods per year

Eggs: 4–7; off-white with dark markings

Incubation: 16–17 days; female incubates

Fledging: 17–21 days; female and male feed the young

Migration: non-migrator in Arizona

Food: insects, lizards, small mammals, frogs

Compare: The Northern Mockingbird (p. 281) has a similar color pattern, but it lacks the black mask. The Cedar Waxwing (p. 149) has a black mask, but it is a brown bird, not gray and black like the Loggerhead Shrike.

Stan's Notes: The Loggerhead is a songbird that acts like a bird of prey. Known for skewering prey on barbed wire fences, thorns and other sharp objects to store or hold still while tearing apart to eat, hence its other common name, Butcher Bird. Feet are too weak to hold the prey it eats. Breeding bird surveys indicate declining populations in many places due to pesticides killing its major food source—grasshoppers. Populations increase during winter when shrikes from northern states migrate to Arizona joining resident birds.

Pyrrhuloxia
Cardinalis sinuatus

YEAR-ROUND

Size: 9" (22.5 cm)

Male: Overall gray with a red mask, throat, breast and belly. Red edges of wings and tail. Bright-red-tipped crest. Stout yellow bill. Dark eyes.

Female: similar to male, lacking red on face, throat, breast and belly, bill is gray to dull yellow

Juvenile: similar to female, has a dark gray bill, lacks red highlights

Nest: cup; female builds; 1 brood per year

Eggs: 2–4; gray to green with brown markings

Incubation: 12–14 days; female and male incubate

Fledging: 8–10 days; female and male feed young

Migration: non-migrator

Food: seeds, fruit, insects; will visit water elements and ground feeders

Compare: Female Northern Cardinal (p. 157) has a black mask and a pointed red bill. Look for the tall crest and thick bill to help identify.

Stan's Notes: This is a secretive bird of arid brush, thorn scrub and mesquite habitat. Like its cousin, the Northern Cardinal, it is most active in early morning and just before sunset. Has a similar loud, crisp song like the cardinal and a single metallic "chip" call. Small flocks move around in the winter to find food. Feeds mostly on the ground, eating grass seeds and insects. Male feeds female during courtship and incubation. Female constructs a nest with twigs and grass in dense shrubs or thickets and lines it with fine grasses and plant fibers. Both defend home territory during the breeding season. Use water elements and ground feeders to attract it to your yard.

American Robin
Turdus migratorius

YEAR-ROUND
WINTER

Size: 9–11" (23–28 cm)

Male: Familiar gray bird with a dark rust-red breast and a nearly black head and tail. White chin with black streaks. White eye-ring.

Female: similar to male, with a duller rust-red breast and a gray head

Juvenile: similar to female, with a speckled breast and brown back

Nest: cup; female builds with help from the male; 2–3 broods per year

Eggs: 4–7; pale blue without markings

Incubation: 12–14 days; female incubates

Fledging: 14–16 days; female and male feed the young

Migration: partial to non-migrator, to southwestern states, and Mexico; non-migrator in half of Arizona

Food: insects, fruit, berries, earthworms

Compare: Familiar bird to all. To differentiate the male from the female, compare the nearly black head and rust-red chest of the male with the gray head and duller chest of the female.

Stan's Notes: Although sometimes a complete migrator in northern states, it is a year-round resident in half of Arizona. Can be heard singing all night long in spring. City robins sing louder than country robins in order to hear one another over traffic and noise. A robin isn't listening for worms when it turns its head to one side. It is focusing its sight out of one eye to look for dirt moving, which is caused by worms moving. Territorial, often fighting its reflection in a window.

displaying

YEAR-ROUND

Northern Mockingbird
Mimus polyglottos

Size: 10" (25 cm)

Male: Silvery-gray head and back with a light-gray breast and belly. White wing patches, seen in flight or during display. Tail mostly black with white outer tail feathers. Black bill.

Female: same as male

Juvenile: dull gray with a heavily streaked breast and a gray bill

Nest: cup; female and male construct; 2 broods per year, sometimes more

Eggs: 3–5; blue-green with brown markings

Incubation: 12–13 days; female incubates

Fledging: 11–13 days; female and male feed the young

Migration: non-migrator in Arizona

Food: insects, fruit

Compare: Loggerhead Shrike (p. 275) has a similar color pattern, but is stockier, has a black mask and perches in more-open places. Townsend's Solitaire (p. 271) has a white eye-ring. Look for Mockingbird to spread its wings, flash its white wing patches and wag its tail from side to side.

Stan's Notes: A very animated bird. Performs an elaborate mating dance. Facing each other with heads and tails erect, pairs will run toward each other, flashing their white wing patches, and then retreat to cover nearby. Thought to flash the wing patches to scare up insects when hunting. Sits for long periods on top of shrubs. Imitates other birds (vocal mimicry); hence the common name. Young males often sing at night. Often unafraid of people, allowing for close observation.

male

female

Gambel's Quail
Callipepla gambelii

YEAR-ROUND

Size: 10" (25 cm)

Male: A plump round bird with a short tail. Gray chest, back and tail. Rusty crest outlined in white. Dark chin, throat and forehead with a unique dark plume emanating from the forehead. Rusty sides with white streaks. A dark patch on belly. Black bill. Gray legs.

Female: similar to male, lacks a rusty crest and dark chin, throat and forehead, plume less robust

Juvenile: similar to female

Nest: ground; female builds; 1–2 broods per year

Eggs: 8–12; dull white with brown markings

Incubation: 21–24 days; female incubates

Fledging: 7–10 days; female and male show the young what to eat

Migration: non-migrator

Food: seeds, leaves, insects, fruit; comes to seed feeders on the ground

Compare: Same size as Scaled Quail (p. 285). Look for Gambel's unique plume to help identify.

Stan's Notes: A native species. Prefers arid scrubby regions with a constant water source. Winter flocks of up to 20 birds (coveys) split up during breeding season. Covey walks in single file. Able to hop on and over fences. Scurries across open areas to reach cover. Visits feeders in early morning and late afternoon. Takes dust baths in dirt depressions, kicking dust over body to get rid of small insects. Builds cup nest under vegetation, lining it with grass and feathers. Male gives a distinctive, repeating call, "yup-waay-yup-yup."

YEAR-ROUND

Scaled Quail
Callipepla squamata

Size: 10" (25 cm)

Male: Overall gray with a prominent white-tipped crest. Scaly appearance due to black-tipped feathers on gray neck, chest and belly. Short gray tail. Small black bill. Dark eyes. Gray legs and feet.

Female: same as male

Juvenile: similar to adult

Nest: ground; female builds; 1 brood per year

Eggs: 12–14; white with or without markings

Incubation: 21–23 days; female incubates

Fledging: 3–7 days; female and male show the young what to eat

Migration: non-migrator

Food: seeds, leaves, insects, fruit; comes to seed feeders on the ground

Compare: Gambel's Quail (pg. 283) has a plume on forehead and longer tail. Scaled Quail lacks the male Gambel's black throat patch. Look for the white-tipped crest to help identify.

Stan's Notes: Similar activities and behaviors as Gambel's Quail. Hybridizes with Gambel's Quails where large populations overlap. Forms large winter flocks of up to 100 birds called coveys. Smaller groups in summer. Dominant males perch on elevated perches to watch for predators. Unmated males call from perches, looking for females. Male raises crest and droops wings for female during courtship. Female scrapes a depression in the ground in tall grass or under shrubs and lines nest with dried grass and a few feathers.

Curve-billed Thrasher

Toxostoma curvirostre

YEAR-ROUND

Size: 11" (28 cm)

Male: Overall gray to light-brown large-bodied bird with a long tail. Faint spots on breast and belly. Long downward-curved bill. Dark-yellow-to-orange eyes.

Female: same as male

Juvenile: similar to adult, with a shorter bill

Nest: cup; female and male construct; 1–2 broods per year

Eggs: 3–4; pale blue-green with brown markings

Incubation: 12–14 days; female and male incubate

Fledging: 14–18 days; female and male feed young

Migration: non-migrator

Food: insects, fruit, seeds; comes to seed feeders on the ground and water elements

Compare: The Sage Thrasher (p. 269) has obvious streaks on the chest. Cactus Wren (p. 159) is smaller and has a spotty dark patch on the chest and a chestnut-brown cap.

Stan's Notes: A familiar backyard bird that prefers scrubby desert habitat with mesquite, cholla and other cactus. Will drive out any Cactus Wrens in its territory. Calls a loud, two-syllable "whit-wee." Feeds on the ground. Male follows female during courtship, singing a soft song. Builds nest in a spiny shrub or cactus, using twigs and grass and lining it with finer plant material. Will often reuse the nest after making minor repairs. Pairs often remain together all year. Young hatch on sequential days, requiring the parents to brood young for more than two weeks. In hot weather parents shade the young from sun.

White-winged Dove
Zenaida asiatica

YEAR-ROUND
SUMMER

Size: 11" (28 cm)

Male: Light-gray-to-brown dove. A conspicuous white edge on the wings. Small black dash underneath the cheeks. Vivid blue eye-rings around bright-red eyes. Black wing tips with a white patch across the middle of wings, as seen in flight.

Female: same as male

Juvenile: similar to adult

Nest: platform; female and male build; 2–3 broods per year

Eggs: 2–4; white without markings

Incubation: 13–14 days; female and male incubate

Fledging: 13–16 days; female and male feed young

Migration: partial migrator to non-migrator

Food: seeds, fruit; will come to seed feeders

Compare: Mourning Dove (p. 183) is slightly larger and lacks the white line on closed wings and a white-and-black pattern in flight.

Stan's Notes: Very similar to the Mourning Dove in behavior and appearance. Feeds on the ground, pecking at seeds and tiny grains of rock to aid digestion. Parents feed young a regurgitated liquid called crop-milk the first few days of life. Male uses its white-and-black wing coloration to display to mate. May nest alone or in large colonies. This non-native species was introduced during the 1950s when captive birds were released in Florida. Gives a distinctive call, "coo-cuk-ca-roo."

YEAR-ROUND

Clark's Nutcracker
Nucifraga columbiana

Size: 12" (30 cm)

Male: Gray with black wings and a narrow black band down the center of tail. Small white patches on long wings, seen in flight. Has a relatively short tail with a white undertail.

Female: same as male

Juvenile: same as adult

Nest: cup; female and male build; 1 brood a year

Eggs: 2–5; pale green with brown markings

Incubation: 16–18 days; female incubates

Fledging: 14–15 days; male and female feed young

Migration: non-migrator

Food: seeds, insects, berries, eggs, mammals

Compare: Townsend's Solitaire (p. 271) is smaller, lacks black wings and has a smaller bill. The Steller's Jay (p. 99) is dark blue with a black crest. Female Phainopepla (p. 267) has a crest and lacks a white undertail.

Stan's Notes: A high-country bird found in coniferous forests in parts of Arizona. It has a varied diet but relies heavily on pinyon seeds, frequently caching large amounts to consume later or feed to young. Has a large pouch under its tongue (sublingual pouch), which it uses to transport seeds. Studies show the birds can carry up to 100 seeds at a time. Nests early in the year, often while snow still covers the ground, relying on stored foods. A "Lewis and Clark" bird, first recorded by William Clark in 1805 in Idaho.

Eurasian Collared-Dove
Streptopelia decaocto

YEAR-ROUND

Size: 12½" (32 cm)

Male: Head, neck, breast and belly are gray to tan. Back, wings and tail are slightly darker. Thin black collar with a white border on the nape of the neck. Tail is long and squared.

Female: same as male

Juvenile: similar to adults

Nest: platform; female and male build; 2–3 broods per year

Eggs: 3–5; creamy white without markings

Incubation: 12–14 days; female and male incubate

Fledging: 12–14 days; female and male feed the young

Migration: non-migrator

Food: seeds; will visit ground and seed feeders

Compare: The Mourning Dove (p. 183) is slightly smaller and darker. The Rock Pigeon (p. 295) has colorful iridescent patches. White-winged Dove (p. 289) has a white line on closed wings and a white-and-black pattern in flight. Look for the black collar on the nape and the squared tail to help identify the Eurasian Collared-Dove.

Stan's Notes: This non-native bird has spread into Arizona, having moved into Florida in the early 1980s after inadvertent introduction to the Bahamas. It has been expanding its range across North America and is predicted to spread just like it did through Europe from Asia. Unknown how this "new" bird will affect populations of the native Mourning Dove. Nearly identical to the Ringed Turtle-Dove, a common pet bird. The dark mark on the back of the neck gave rise to the common name. Look for flashes of white in the tail and dark wing tips when it lands or takes off.

Rock Pigeon
Columba livia

YEAR-ROUND

Size: 13" (33 cm)

Male: No set color pattern. Shades of gray to white with patches of gleaming, iridescent green and blue. Often has a light rump patch.

Female: same as male

Juvenile: same as adults

Nest: platform; female builds; 3–4 broods per year

Eggs: 1–2; white without markings

Incubation: 18–20 days; female and male incubate

Fledging: 25–26 days; female and male feed the young

Migration: non-migrator

Food: seeds

Compare: The Mourning Dove (p. 183) is smaller and light brown and lacks the variety of color combinations of the Rock Pigeon.

Stan's Notes: Also known as the Domestic Pigeon. Formerly known as the Rock Dove. Introduced to North America from Europe by the early settlers. Most common around cities and barnyards, where it scratches for seeds. One of the few birds with a wide variety of colors, produced by years of selective breeding while in captivity. Parents feed the young a regurgitated liquid known as crop-milk for the first few days of life. One of the few birds that can drink without tilting its head back. Nests under bridges or on buildings, balconies, barns and sheds. Was once thought to be a nuisance in cities and was poisoned. Now, many cities have Peregrine Falcons (p. 301) feeding on Rock Pigeons, which keeps their numbers in check.

soaring

juvenile

Sharp-shinned Hawk

Accipiter striatus

YEAR-ROUND
WINTER

Size: 10–14" (25–36 cm); up to 2' wingspan

Male: Small woodland hawk with a gray back and head and a rust-red chest. Short wings. Long, squared tail and several dark tail bands, with the widest at the end of the tail. Red eyes.

Female: same as male but larger

Juvenile: same size as adults, with a brown back, heavy streaking on the chest and yellow eyes

Nest: platform; female builds; 1 brood per year

Eggs: 4–5; white with brown markings

Incubation: 32–35 days; female incubates

Fledging: 24–27 days; female and male feed the young

Migration: partial to non-migrator, to southwestern states, Mexico and Central America; non-migrator in parts of Arizona

Food: birds, small mammals

Compare: Cooper's Hawk (p. 299) is larger and has a larger head, a slightly longer neck and a rounded tail. Look for the squared tail to help identify the Sharp-shinned Hawk.

Stan's Notes: A common hawk of backyards, parks and woodlands. Seen swooping on birds visiting feeders and chasing them as they flee. Its short wingspan and long tail help it to maneuver through thick stands of trees in pursuit of prey. Calls a loud, high-pitched "kik-kik-kik-kik." Named "Sharp-shinned" for the sharp projection (keel) on the leading edge of its shin. A bird's shin is actually below the ankle (rather than above it, like ours) on the tarsus bone of its foot. In most birds, the tarsus bone is rounded, not sharp.

soaring

juvenile

Cooper's Hawk
Accipiter cooperii

Size: 14–20" (36–51 cm); up to 3' wingspan

Male: Medium-size hawk with short wings and a long, rounded tail with several black bands. Slate-gray back, rusty breast, dark wing tips. Gray bill with a bright-yellow spot at the base. Dark-red eyes.

Female: similar to male but larger

Juvenile: brown back, brown streaking on the breast, bright-yellow eyes

Nest: platform; male and female construct; 1 brood per year

Eggs: 2–4; greenish with brown markings

Incubation: 32–36 days; female and male incubate

Fledging: 28–32 days; male and female feed the young

Migration: non-migrator to partial migrator; will move around to find food

Food: small birds, mammals

Compare: Sharp-shinned Hawk (p. 297) is much smaller, lighter gray and has a squared tail. Look for the banded, rounded tail to help identify Cooper's Hawk.

Stan's Notes: Resident hawk in much of Arizona. Found in many habitats, from woodlands to parks and backyards. In flight, look for its large head, short wings and long tail. The stubby wings help it to navigate around trees while it chases small birds. Will ambush prey, flying into heavy brush or even running on the ground. Comes to feeders, hunting for birds. Flies with long glides followed by a few quick flaps. Calls a loud, clear "cack-cack-cack-cack." The young have gray eyes that turn bright yellow at 1 year and turn dark red later, after 3–5 years.

juvenile

in-flight
juvenile

in flight

Peregrine Falcon
Falco peregrinus

Size: 16–20" (41–51 cm); up to 3¾' wingspan

Male: Dark-gray back and tan-to-white chest. Horizontal bars on belly, legs and undertail. Dark "hood" head marking and wide black mustache. Yellow base of bill and eye-ring. Yellow legs.

Female: similar to male but noticeably larger

Juvenile: overall darker than adults, with heavy streaking on the chest and belly

Nest: ground (scrape) on a cliff edge, tall building, bridge or smokestack; 1 brood per year

Eggs: 3–4; white, some with brown markings

Incubation: 29–32 days; female and male incubate

Fledging: 35–42 days; male and female feed the young

Migration: partial to non-migrator; moves around to find food

Food: birds (Rock Pigeons in cities, shorebirds and waterfowl in rural areas)

Compare: The American Kestrel (p. 173) is smaller and has 2 vertical black stripes on its face. Look for the dark "hood" head marking and mustache marks to identify the Peregrine Falcon.

Stan's Notes: A wide-bodied raptor that hunts many bird species. The larger females hunt larger prey. Lives in many cities, diving (stooping) on pigeons at speeds of up to 200 miles (322 km) per hour, which knocks them to the ground. Soars with its wings flat, often riding thermals. During courtship, the male brings food to the female and performs aerial displays. Likes to nest on a high ledge or platform for a good view of its territory. A solitary nester and monogamous.

female
p. 207

male

soaring

Northern Harrier
Circus hudsonius

YEAR-ROUND WINTER

Size: 18–22" (45–56 cm); up to 4' wingspan

Male: Slender, low-flying hawk. Silver-gray with a large white rump patch and white belly. Long tail with faint narrow bands. Black wing tips. Yellow eyes.

Female: dark-brown back, brown streaking on breast and belly, large white rump patch, thin black tail bands, black wing tips, yellow eyes

Juvenile: similar to female, with an orange breast

Nest: ground; female and male construct; 1 brood per year

Eggs: 4–8; bluish white without markings

Incubation: 31–32 days; female incubates

Fledging: 30–35 days; male and female feed the young

Migration: partial to complete, to Arizona, southwestern states, Mexico and Central America

Food: mice, snakes, insects, small birds

Compare: Slimmer than the Red-tailed Hawk (p. 211). Cooper's Hawk (p. 299) has a rusty breast. Look for a low-gliding hawk with a large white rump patch to identify the male Harrier.

Stan's Notes: One of the easiest of hawks to identify. Glides just above the ground, following the contours of the land while searching for prey. Holds its wings just above horizontal, tilting back and forth in the wind, similar to Turkey Vultures. Formerly called the Marsh Hawk due to its habit of hunting over marshes. Feeds and nests on the ground. Will also preen and rest on the ground. Unlike other hawks, mainly uses its hearing to find prey, followed by sight. At any age, has a distinctive owl-like face disk.

female
p. 197

male

Gadwall
Mareca strepera

Size: 20" (48 cm)

Male: A plump gray duck with a brown head and a distinctive black rump. White belly. Chestnut-tinged wings. Bright-white wing linings. Small white wing patch, seen when swimming. Gray bill.

Female: similar to female Mallard, a mottled brown with a pronounced color change from dark-brown body to light-brown neck and head, bright-white wing linings, small white wing patch, gray bill with orange sides

Juvenile: similar to female

Nest: ground; female lines the nest with fine grass and down feathers plucked from her chest; 1 brood per year

Eggs: 8–11; white without markings

Incubation: 24–27 days; female incubates

Fledging: 48–56 days; young feed themselves

Migration: complete, to Arizona, southwestern states and Mexico

Food: aquatic insects

Compare: Male Gadwall is one of the few gray ducks. Look for its distinctive black rump.

Stan's Notes: A duck of shallow marshes. Consumes mostly plant material, dunking its head in water to feed rather than tipping forward, like other dabbling ducks. Frequently in pairs with other duck species. Nests within 300 feet (90 m) of water. Establishes pair bond in winter. Doesn't nest in Arizona.

in flight

Canada Goose
Branta canadensis

WINTER

Size:	25–43" (64–109 cm); up to 5½' wingspan
Male:	Large gray goose with a black neck and head. White chin and cheek strap.
Female:	same as male
Juvenile:	same as adults
Nest:	platform, on the ground; female builds; 1 brood per year
Eggs:	5–10; white without markings
Incubation:	25–30 days; female incubates
Fledging:	42–55 days; male and female teach the young to feed
Migration:	partial to complete migrator, to Arizona and other southwestern states; will move to any place with open water
Food:	aquatic plants, insects, seeds
Compare:	Large goose that is rarely confused with any other bird.

Stan's Notes: A winter resident in Arizona. Flocks fly in a large V when traveling long distances. Begins breeding in the third year. Adults mate for many years. If threatened, they will hiss as a warning. Males stand as sentinels at the edge of their group and will bob their heads and become aggressive if approached. Adults molt their primary flight feathers while raising their young, rendering family groups temporarily flightless. Several subspecies occur in the U.S. Generally eastern groups are paler than western. Their size also varies, decreasing northward. The smallest sub-species is in the Arctic.

in flight

Great Blue Heron
Ardea herodias

YEAR-ROUND

Size: 42–48" (107–122 cm); up to 6' wingspan

Male: Tall and gray. Black eyebrows end in long plumes at the back of the head. Long yellow bill. Long feathers at the base of the neck drop down in a kind of necklace. Long legs.

Female: same as male

Juvenile: same as adults, but more brown than gray, with a black crown; lacks plumes

Nest: platform in a colony; male and female build; 1 brood per year

Eggs: 3–5; blue-green without markings

Incubation: 27–28 days; female and male incubate

Fledging: 56–60 days; male and female feed the young

Migration: non-migrator in Arizona

Food: small fish, frogs, insects, snakes, baby birds

Compare: The Sandhill Crane (p. 311) has a red cap. Look for the long, yellow bill to help identify the Great Blue Heron.

Stan's Notes: One of the most common herons. Found in open water, from small ponds to large lakes. Stalks small fish in shallow water. Will strike at mice, squirrels and nearly anything it comes across. Red-winged Blackbirds will attack it to stop it from taking their babies out of the nest. In flight, it holds its neck in an S shape and slightly cups its wings, while the legs trail straight out behind. Nests in a colony of up to 100 birds. Nests in trees near or hanging over water. Barks like a dog when startled. Populations increase in winter when birds from northern states join resident birds.

in flight

rusty stain

in-flight
rusty stain

Sandhill Crane

Grus canadensis

Size: 42–48" (107–122 cm); up to 7' wingspan

Male: Elegant gray crane with long legs and neck. Wings and body often rust brown from mud staining. Scarlet-red cap. Yellow to red eyes.

Female: same as male

Juvenile: dull brown with yellow eyes; lacks a red cap

Nest: ground; female and male construct; 1 brood per year

Eggs: 2; olive with brown markings

Incubation: 28–32 days; female and male incubate

Fledging: 65 days; female and male feed the young

Migration: complete, to parts of Arizona, Mexico

Food: insects, fruit, worms, plants, amphibians

Compare: Great Blue Heron (p. 309) has a longer bill and holds its neck in an S shape during flight. Look for the scarlet-red cap to help identify the Sandhill Crane.

MIGRATION
WINTER

Stan's Notes: Preens mud into its feathers, staining its plumage rust brown (see insets). Gives a very loud and distinctive rattling call, often heard before the bird is seen. Flight is characteristic, with a faster upstroke, making the wings look like they're flicking in flight. Can fly at heights of over 10,000 feet (3,050 m). Nests on the ground in a large mound of aquatic vegetation. Performs a spectacular mating dance: The birds will face each other, then bow and jump into the air while making loud cackling sounds and flapping their wings. They will also flip sticks and grass into the air during their dance.

male

female

Costa's Hummingbird

Calypte costae

YEAR-ROUND
SUMMER

Size: 3½" (9 cm)

Male: Green back and nape. White belly. Light-green flanks. Dark crown, chin, throat and down the neck, like a handlebar mustache. White eyebrows. In direct sunlight, dark area around head reflects iridescent purple.

Female: same as male, without dark marks on head, has white marks around eyes, gray cheeks

Juvenile: similar to female

Nest: cup; female builds; 1 brood per year

Eggs: 2; white without markings

Incubation: 15–18 days; female incubates

Fledging: 20–23 days; female feeds young

Migration: partial migrator to non-migrator, to Mexico

Food: small insects, flower nectar; visits feeders

Compare: Smaller than the other hummers in Arizona and has a shorter tail than most. Look for male's purple cap and mustache marks on throat. Identify the female by its gray cheeks and white markings around each eye. Wings extend just beyond tip of tail when perched.

Stan's Notes: Good lighting is needed to see the green iridescence. Some stay the winter if a consistent food source is available, such as a hummingbird feeder. Actively defends itself and is very territorial. Often perches, guarding territory and food supply. Gives a limited song, "tink-tink-tink," as it chases other hummers. Male performs an elaborate diving flight display to attract a mate. After mating, the female moves to her own territory to build nest and raise young.

male

female

SUMMER

Black-chinned Hummingbird
Archilochus alexandri

Size: 3¾" (9.5 cm)

Male: Tiny iridescent green bird with black throat patch (gorget) that reflects violet-blue in sunlight. Black chin. White chest and belly.

Female: same as male, but lacking the throat patch and black chin, has white flanks

Juvenile: similar to female

Nest: cup; female builds; 1–2 broods per year

Eggs: 1–3; white without markings

Incubation: 13–16 days; female incubates

Fledging: 19–21 days; female feeds young

Migration: complete, to Central and South America

Food: nectar, insects; will come to nectar feeders

Compare: Male Broad-tailed Hummingbird (p. 317) is slightly larger and has a rosy-red throat patch and lacks a black chin. The flanks of female Broad-tailed (p. 317) are tan, not white, like those of the female Black-chinned.

Stan's Notes: One of the smallest birds in Arizona and one of several hummingbird species in the state, these are the only birds with the ability to fly backward. Doesn't sing. Will chatter or buzz to communicate. Wings create a humming noise, flapping nearly 80 times per second. Weighing only 2–3 grams, it takes approximately five average-sized hummingbirds to equal the weight of one chickadee. Males return first at the end of April. Male performs a spectacular pendulum-like flight over a perched female. After mating, the female builds a nest, using spiderwebs to glue nest materials together, and raises young without the mate's help. More than one clutch per year not uncommon.

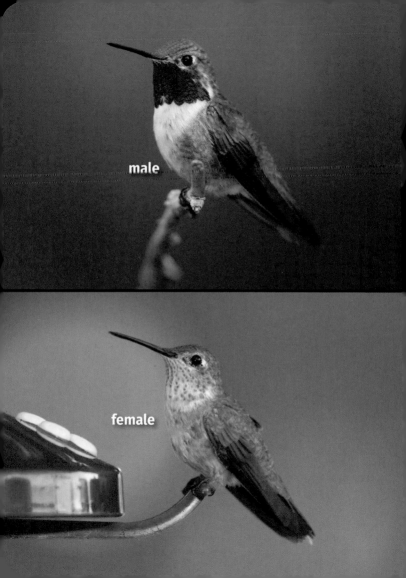

SUMMER

Broad-tailed Hummingbird
Selasphorus platycercus

Size: 4" (10 cm)

Male: Tiny iridescent green bird with a black throat patch (gorget) that reflects rosy red in sunlight. Wings and part of the back are green. White chest.

Female: same as male, but lacking the throat patch, much more green on back, tan flanks

Juvenile: similar to female

Nest: cup; female builds; 1–2 broods per year

Eggs: 1–3; white without markings

Incubation: 12–14 days; female incubates

Fledging: 20–22 days; female feeds young

Migration: complete, to Mexico and Central America

Food: nectar, insects; will come to nectar feeders

Compare: The male Black-chinned Hummingbird (p. 315) is slightly smaller and has a violet-blue throat patch and a black chin. Female Black-chinned (p. 315) has white flanks, unlike the tan flanks of female Broad-tailed.

Stan's Notes: Hummingbirds are the only birds with the ability to fly backward. Does not sing. Will chatter or buzz to communicate. Wingbeats produce a whistle, almost like a tiny ringing bell. Heart pumps up to an incredible 1,260 beats every minute. Weighing just 2–3 grams, it takes about five average-sized hummingbirds to equal the weight of one chickadee. Male performs a spectacular pendulum-like flight over the perched female. After mating, female builds the nest and raises young without any help from her mate. Constructs a soft, flexible nest that expands to accommodate the growing young.

Anna's Hummingbird

Calypte anna

YEAR-ROUND
WINTER

Size: 4" (10 cm)

Male: Iridescent green body with dark head, chin and neck. In direct sunlight, the dark head shines a deep rose-red. Breast and belly are dull gray. White eye-ring.

Female: similar to male, but head reflects only a few red flecks instead of a complete rose-red

Juvenile: similar to female

Nest: cup; female builds; 2–3 broods per year

Eggs: 1–3; white without markings

Incubation: 14–19 days; female incubates

Fledging: 18–23 days; female feeds the young

Migration: partial migrator to non-migrator; many move to the coast of southern California and Mexico

Food: nectar, insects; will come to nectar feeders

Compare: Anna's is similar to other hummingbirds, but male has a completely dark head and a white eye-ring. Female has a few red flecks on the throat. Tail extends well beyond the wing tips when perched.

Stan's Notes: Common western hummingbird found from Baja California, to British Columbia. Unknown in the state before the late 1950s, it has since expanded northward and is now considered common. An early nester. Female builds a tiny nest on chaparral-covered hillsides and in canyons. Feathers on head are black until seen in direct sun. Reflected sunlight turns the male's head bright rosy red. Apparently consumes more insects than other species of hummingbirds.

male

female

Violet-green Swallow
Tachycineta thalassina

SUMMER
MIGRATION

Size: 5¼" (13.5 cm)

Male: Dull emerald green crown, nape and back. Violet-blue wings and tail. White chest and belly. White cheeks with white extending above the eyes. Wings extend beyond the tail when perching.

Female: same as male, only duller

Juvenile: similar to adult of the same sex

Nest: cavity; female and male build nest in tree cavities, old woodpecker holes; 1 brood per year

Eggs: 4–6; pale white with brown markings

Incubation: 13–14 days; female incubates

Fledging: 18–24 days; female and male feed the young

Migration: complete, to Mexico and Central America

Food: insects

Compare: Similar size as the Cliff Swallow (p. 123), which has a distinctive tan-to-rust pattern on the head. Barn Swallow (p. 89) has a distinctive, deeply forked tail.

Stan's Notes: A solitary nester in tree cavities and rarely beneath cliff overhangs. Can be attracted with a nest box. Will search for miles for loose feathers to line its nest. Tail is short and wing tips extend beyond the end of it, seen when perching. Returns to Arizona in April and begins nesting right away. Young often leave the nest by June. On cloudy days they look black, but on sunny days they look metallic green.

Green-tailed Towhee
Pipilo chlorurus

SUMMER
MIGRATION
WINTER

Size: 7¼" (18.5 cm)

Male: A unique yellowish-green back, wings and tail. Dark-gray chest and face. Bright-white throat with black stripes. Rusty-red crown.

Female: same as male

Juvenile: olive-green with heavy streaking on breast and belly, lacks crown and throat markings of adult

Nest: cup; female and male construct; 1–2 broods per year

Eggs: 3–5; white with brown markings

Incubation: 12–14 days; female and male incubate

Fledging: 10–14 days; female and male feed young

Migration: to: complete, to southern Arizona, other southwestern states and Mexico

Food: insects, seeds, fruit

Compare: Canyon Towhee (p. 167) has a distinctive necklace of dark spots. The Abert's Towhee (p. 169) lacks the Green-tailed's rusty-red crown and bright-white throat. The Green-tailed's unusual color, short wings, long tail and large bill make it easy to identify.

Stan's Notes: A common bird of shrubby hillsides and sagebrush mountain slopes as high as 7,000 feet (2,150 m). Like other towhees, searches for insects and seeds, taking a little jump forward while kicking backward with both feet. Known to scurry away from trouble, jumping to ground without opening its wings and running across the ground.

Lewis's Woodpecker
Melanerpes lewis

YEAR-ROUND
WINTER

Size: 10¾" (27.5 cm)

Male: Dull-green head and back. Distinctive gray collar and breast. Deep-red face and a light-red belly.

Female: same as male

Juvenile: similar to adult, with a brown head, lacking the red face

Nest: cavity; male and female excavate; 1 brood per year

Eggs: 4–8; white without markings

Incubation: 13–14 days; female and male incubate

Fledging: 28–34 days; female and male feed young

Migration: non-migrator to partial migrator; will move around to find food in winter

Food: insects, nuts, seeds, berries

Compare: Acorn Woodpecker (p. 69) has white on head and a red cap. Red-naped Sapsucker (p. 63) has a black-and-white pattern on back and much more red on the head.

Stan's Notes: Large and handsome woodpecker of western states. First scientifically collected in 1805 by Lewis and Clark in Montana. During breeding season, it feeds exclusively on adult insects rather than grubs, like other woodpeckers. Prefers open pine forests and areas with recent forest fires. Excavates in dead or soft wood. Uses same cavity year after year. Tends to mate for a long term. Doesn't migrate, but moves around in winter to search for food, such as pine nuts (seeds).

in flight

Green Heron
Butorides virescens

Size: 16–22" (41–56 cm)

Male: Short and stocky. Blue-green back and rust-red neck and breast. Dark-green crest. Short legs are normally yellow but turn bright orange during the breeding season.

Female: same as male

Juvenile: similar to adults, with a bluish-gray back and white-streaked breast and neck

Nest: platform; female and male build; 2 broods per year

Eggs: 2–4; light green without markings

Incubation: 21–25 days; female and male incubate

Fledging: 35–36 days; female and male feed the young

Migration: complete, to Mexico, Central America and South America; some are non-migrators in parts of southern Arizona

Food: small fish, aquatic insects, small amphibians

Compare: Great Blue Heron (p. 309) is larger. Green Heron lacks the long neck of other herons. Look for a small heron with a dark-green back and crest to identify the Green.

Stan's Notes: Often gives an explosive, rasping "skyew" call when startled. Holds its head close to its body, which sometimes makes it look like it doesn't have a neck. Waits on the shore or wades stealthily, hunting for small fish, aquatic insects and small amphibians. Places an object, such as an insect, on the water's surface to attract fish to catch. Nests in a tall tree, often a short distance from the water. The nest can be very high up in the tree. Babies give a loud ticking sound, like the ticktock of a clock.

female
p. 203

male

Mallard
Anas platyrhynchos

YEAR-ROUND

Size: 19–21" (48–53 cm)

Male: Large, bulbous green head, white necklace and rust-brown or chestnut chest. Gray-and-white sides. Yellow bill. Orange legs and feet.

Female: brown with an orange-and-black bill and blue-and-white wing mark (speculum)

Juvenile: same as female but with a yellow bill

Nest: ground; female builds; 1 brood per year

Eggs: 7–10; greenish to whitish, unmarked

Incubation: 26–30 days; female incubates

Fledging: 42–52 days; female leads the young to food

Migration: non-migrator to partial migrator in Arizona

Food: seeds, plants, aquatic insects; will come to ground feeders offering corn

Compare: Male Northern Shoveler (p. 331) has a white chest with rusty sides and a very large, spoon-shaped bill. Breeding male Northern Pintail (p. 205) has long tail feathers and a brown head. Look for the green head and yellow bill to identify the male Mallard.

Stan's Notes: A familiar dabbling duck of lakes and ponds. Also found in rivers, streams and some backyards. Tips forward to feed on vegetation on the bottom of shallow water. The name "Mallard" comes from the Latin word *masculus,* meaning "male," referring to the male's habit of taking no part in raising the young. Male and female have white underwings and white tails, but only the male has black central tail feathers that curl upward. Unlike the female, the male doesn't quack.

female
p. 201

male

Northern Shoveler
Anas clypeata

MIGRATION
WINTER

Size: 19–21" (48–53 cm)

Male: Medium-sized duck with an iridescent green head, rust sides, white chest. Extraordinarily large, spoon-shaped bill, almost always held pointed toward the water.

Female: brown and black all over, green wing patch (speculum) and a large spoon-shaped bill

Juvenile: same as female

Nest: ground; female builds; 1 brood per year

Eggs: 9–12; olive without markings

Incubation: 22–25 days; female incubates

Fledging: 30–60 days; female leads the young to food

Migration: complete migrator, to Arizona, Mexico, and Central America

Food: aquatic insects, plants

Compare: Male Mallard (p. 329) is similar, but it lacks the large spoon-shaped bill.

Stan's Notes: One of several species of shovelers. Called "Shoveler" due to the peculiar, shovel-like shape of its bill. Given the common name "Northern" because it is the only species of these ducks in North America. Seen in shallow wetlands, ponds and small lakes in flocks of 5–10 birds. Flocks fly in tight formation. Swims low in water, pointing its large bill toward the water as if it's too heavy to lift. Usually swims in tight circles while feeding. Feeds mainly by filtering tiny aquatic insects and plants from the surface of the water with its bill. Female gathers plant material and forms it into a nest a short distance from the water.

female
p. 369

male

Bullock's Oriole
Icterus bullockii

Size: 8" (20 cm)

Male: Bright-orange-and-black bird. Black crown, eye line, nape, chin, back and wings with a bold white patch on wings.

Female: dull-yellow overall, pale-white belly, white wing bars on gray-to-black wings

Juvenile: similar to female

Nest: pendulous; female and male build; 1 brood per year

Eggs: 4–6; pale white to gray, brown markings

Incubation: 12–14 days; female incubates

Fledging: 12–14 days; female and male feed young

Migration: complete, to Mexico and Central America

Food: insects, berries, nectar; visits nectar feeders

Compare: A handsome bird. Look for male Bullock's bright orange and black markings, and the thin black line running through the eyes.

Stan's Notes: So closely related to Baltimore Orioles of the eastern U.S., at one time both were considered a single species. Interbreeds with Baltimores where their ranges overlap. Most common in the state where cottonwood trees grow along rivers and other wetlands. Also found at edges of clearings, in city parks, on farms and along irrigation ditches. Hanging sock-like nest is constructed of plant fibers such as inner bark of junipers and willows.

female
p. 155

male

Black-headed Grosbeak
Pheucticus melanocephalus

SUMMER MIGRATION

Size: 8" (20 cm)

Male: Stocky bird with burnt-orange chest, neck and rump. Black head, tail and wings. Irregularly shaped white wing patches. Large bill, with upper bill darker than lower.

Female: appears like an overgrown sparrow, overall brown with a lighter breast and belly, large two-toned bill, prominent white eyebrows, yellow wing linings, as seen in flight

Juvenile: similar to adult of the same sex

Nest: cup; female builds; 1 brood per year

Eggs: 3–4; pale green or bluish, brown markings

Incubation: 11–13 days; female and male incubate

Fledging: 11–13 days; female and male feed young

Migration: complete, to Mexico

Food: seeds, insects, fruit; comes to seed feeders

Compare: Male Evening Grosbeak (p. 371) is the same size, but it has an orange breast and lacks a yellow belly. Male Bullock's Oriole (p. 369) has more white on the wings than the male Black-headed Grosbeak. Look for Black-headed's large bicolored bill.

Stan's Notes: A cosmopolitan bird that nests in a wide variety of habitats. Both the male and female sing and will aggressively defend the nest against intruders. Song is very similar to American Robin's (p. 279) and Western Tanager's (p. 365), making it hard to tell them apart by song. Populations increasing in Arizona and across the U.S.

male

female
p. 111

yellow
male

House Finch

Haemorhous mexicanus

YEAR-ROUND

Size: 5" (13 cm)

Male: Small finch with a red-to-orange face, throat, chest and rump. Brown cap. Brown marking behind eyes. White belly with brown streaks. Brown wings with white streaks.

Female: brown with a heavily streaked white chest

Juvenile: similar to female

Nest: cup, sometimes in cavities; female builds; 2 broods per year

Eggs: 4–5; pale blue, lightly marked

Incubation: 12–14 days; female incubates

Fledging: 15–19 days; female and male feed the young

Migration: non-migrator to partial migrator; moves around to find food

Food: seeds, fruit, leaf buds; visits seed feeders and feeders that offer grape jelly

Compare: The male Northern Cardinal (p. 343) has a crest and black mask. The male Vermilion Flycatcher (p. 339) has a black nape, back and wings.

Stan's Notes: Very social bird, visits feeders in small flocks. Likes to nest in hanging flower baskets. Male sings a loud, cheerful warbling song. Historically it occurred from the Pacific to the Rockies, with only a few reaching the eastern side. Now found across the U.S. Suffers from a disease that causes the eyes to crust, resulting in blindness and death. Rarely, some males are yellow (see inset) instead of red, probably due to poor diet.

male

female
p. 257

Vermilion Flycatcher
Pyrocephalus rubinus

YEAR-ROUND
SUMMER

Size: 6" (15 cm)

Male: A stunningly beautiful bird with a crimson-red head, crest, chin, breast and belly. Black nape, back, wings and tail. Thick black line running through eyes. Thin black bill.

Female: gray head, neck and back, nearly white chin and breast, pink belly to undertail, black tail, thin black bill

Juvenile: similar to female, lacks a pink undertail

Nest: cup; female builds; 1–2 broods per year

Eggs: 2–4; white with brown markings

Incubation: 14–16 days; female and male incubate

Fledging: 14–16 days; female and male feed young

Migration: partial migrator, to southern Arizona, throughout Mexico; non-migrator in parts of Arizona

Food: insects (mainly bees)

Compare: The unique bright crimson plumage with black wings make this bird easy to identify.

Stan's Notes: A uniquely colored flycatcher that is often found in open areas with shrubs and small trees close to water. Feeds mainly on insects, with bees making up a large part of its diet. Will perch on a thin branch, pumping tail up and down while waiting for an aerial insect. Flies out to snatch it, then returns to the perch. Drops to the ground for terrestrial insects. Male raises its crest, fluffs chest feathers, fans tail and sings a song during a fluttery flight to court females. Female builds a shallow nest of twigs and grasses and lines it with downy plant material. Male feeds female during incubation and brooding.

female
p. 367

male

Summer Tanager
Piranga rubra

Size: 8" (20 cm)

Male: Bright rosy-red bird with darker-red wings.

Female: overall yellow with slightly darker wings

Juvenile: male has patches of red and green over the entire body, female is same as adult female

Nest: cup; female builds; 1–2 broods per year

Eggs: 3–5; pale blue with dark markings

Incubation: 10–12 days; female incubates

Fledging: 12–15 days; female and male feed young

Migration: complete, to Central and South America

Food: insects, fruit

Compare: Similar size as the male Northern Cardinal (p. 343), but the male Cardinal has a black mask, large crest and red bill.

Stan's Notes: Found in Arizona where woodlands exist, especially in mixed pine and oak forests. Due to clearing of land for agriculture, populations have decreased for over a century and especially most recently. Returning to the state in late April and with young hatching in late May, some pairs have two broods per year. While fruit makes up some of the diet, most of it consists of insects such as bees and wasps. Summer Tanagers unfortunately seem to be parasitized by Brown-headed and Bronzed Cowbirds.

female
p. 157

male

juvenile

YEAR-ROUND

Northern Cardinal
Cardinalis cardinalis

Size: 8–9" (20–23 cm)

Male: Red with a black mask that extends from the face to the throat. Large crest and a large red bill.

Female: buff-brown with a black mask, large reddish bill, and red tinges on the crest and wings

Juvenile: same as female but with a blackish-gray bill

Nest: cup; female builds; 2–3 broods per year

Eggs: 3–4; bluish white with brown markings

Incubation: 12–13 days; female and male incubate

Fledging: 9–10 days; female and male feed the young

Migration: non-migrator

Food: seeds, insects, fruit; comes to seed feeders

Compare: Similar size as the male Summer Tanager (p. 367), but the Tanager is rosy red. Similar to Pyrrhuloxia (p. 277) but has red bill. Look for Northern Cardinal's black mask, large crest and red bill.

Stan's Notes: A familiar backyard bird in some parts of the state. Seen in a variety of habitats, including parks. Usually likes thick vegetation. One of the few species in which both males and females sing. Can be heard all year. Listen for its "whata-cheer-cheer-cheer" territorial call in spring. Watch for a male feeding a female during courtship. The male also feeds the young of the first brood while the female builds a second nest. Territorial in spring, fighting its own reflection in a window or other reflective surface. Non-territorial in winter, gathering in small flocks of up to 20 birds. Makes short flights from cover to cover, often landing on the ground. *Cardinalis* denotes importance, as represented by the red priestly garments of Catholic cardinals.

female p. 199

male

Redhead
Aythya americana

WINTER

Size: 19" (48 cm)

Male: Rich-red head and neck with a black breast and tail, gray sides, and smoky-gray wings and back. Tricolored bill with a light-blue base, white ring and black tip.

Female: soft-brown, plain-looking duck with gray-to-white wing linings, a rounded top of head and a gray bill with a black tip

Juvenile: similar to female

Nest: cup; female builds; 1 brood per year

Eggs: 9–14; white without markings

Incubation: 24–28 days; female and male incubate

Fledging: 56–73 days; female shows young what to eat

Migration: complete migrator, to Arizona, southwestern states, Mexico and Central America

Food: seeds, aquatic plants, insects

Compare: The male Northern Shoveler (p. 331) has a green head and rusty sides, unlike the red head and gray sides of the male Redhead.

Stan's Notes: A duck of permanent large bodies of water. Forages along the shoreline, feeding on seeds, aquatic plants and insects. Usually builds nest directly on the water's surface, using large mats of vegetation. Female lays up to 75 percent of its eggs in the nests of other Redheads and several other duck species. Nests primarily in the Prairie Pothole region of the northern Great Plains. The overall populations seem to be increasing at about 2–3 percent each year. Winters in Arizona wherever it can find water.

in flight

Snowy Egret
Egretta thula

Size: 22–26" (56–66 cm); up to 3½' wingspan

Male: All-white bird with black bill. Black legs. Bright-yellow feet. Long feather plumes on head, neck and back during breeding season.

Female: same as male

Juvenile: similar to adult, but backs of legs are yellow

Nest: platform; female and male build; 1 brood per year

Eggs: 3–5; light blue-green without markings

Incubation: 20–24 days; female and male incubate

Fledging: 28–30 days; female and male feed the young

Migration: complete migrator to non-migrator, to southern Arizona and Mexico

Food: aquatic insects, small fish

Compare: This is the only all-white egret in Arizona. Look for the black bill and yellow feet of Snowy Egret to help identify.

YEAR-ROUND
MIGRATION
WINTER

Stan's Notes: Common in wetlands and often seen with other egrets. Colonies may include up to several hundred nests. Nests are low in shrubs 5–10 feet (1.5–3 m) tall or constructs a nest on the ground, usually mixed among other egret and heron nests. Chicks hatch days apart (asynchronous), leading to starvation of last to hatch. Will actively "hunt" prey by moving around quickly, stirring up small fish and aquatic insects with its feet. In the breeding state, a yellow patch at the base of bill and the yellow feet turn orange-red. Was hunted to near extinction in the late 1800s for its feathers.

blue morph

juvenile

white
morph

in flight

MIGRATION
WINTER

Snow Goose
Chen caerulescens

Size: 25–38" (64–97 cm); up to 4½' wingspan

Male: White morph has black wing tips and varying patches of black and brown. Blue morph has a white head and a gray breast and back. Both morphs have a pink bill and legs.

Female: same as male

Juvenile: overall dull gray with a dark bill

Nest: ground; female builds; 1 brood per year

Eggs: 3–5; white without markings

Incubation: 23–25 days; female incubates

Fledging: 45–49 days; female and male teach the young to feed

Migration: complete migrator, to southwestern parts of Arizona, California and Mexico

Food: aquatic insects and plants

Compare: The Canada Goose (p. 307) is larger and has a black neck and white chin strap.

Stan's Notes: This bird occurs in light (white) and dark (blue) color morphs. The white morph is more common than the blue. A bird of wide-open fields, wetlands and lakes of any size. It has a thick, serrated bill, which helps it to grab and pull up plants. Breeds in large colonies on the northern tundra in Canada. Female starts to breed at 2–3 years. Older females produce more eggs and are more successful at reproduction than younger females. Seen by the thousands during migration and in winter. Has a classic goose-like call. Often associated with Sandhill Cranes.

in flight

Great Egret
Ardea alba

YEAR-ROUND
MIGRATION
WINTER

Size: 36–40" (91–102 cm); up to 4½' wingspan

Male: Tall, thin, all-white bird with a long neck and a long, pointed yellow bill. Black, stilt-like legs and black feet.

Female: same as male

Juvenile: same as adults

Nest: platform; male and female construct; 1 brood per year

Eggs: 2–3; light blue without markings

Incubation: 23–26 days; female and male incubate

Fledging: 43–49 days; female and male feed the young

Migration: partial to non-migrator

Food: small fish, aquatic insects, frogs, crayfish

Compare: The Snowy Egret (p. 347) is much smaller, with yellow feet and a black bill.

Stan's Notes: Slowly stalks shallow ponds, lakes and wetlands in search of small fish to spear with its long, sharp bill. Gives a loud, dry croak if disturbed or when squabbling for a nest site at the colony. The name "Egret" comes from the French word *aigrette*, meaning "ornamental tufts of plumes." The plumes grow near the tail during the breeding season. Hunted to near extinction in the 1800s and early 1900s for its long plumes, which were used to decorate women's hats. Today, the egret is a protected species.

male

female

Wilson's Warbler
Cardellina pusilla

MIGRATION

Size:	4¾" (12 cm)
Male:	Dull-yellow upper and bright-yellow lower. Distinctive black cap. Large black eyes and small thin bill.
Female:	same as male, but lacking the black cap
Juvenile:	similar to female
Nest:	cup; female builds; 1 brood per year
Eggs:	4–6; white with brown markings
Incubation:	10–13 days; female incubates
Fledging:	8–11 days; female and male feed young
Migration:	complete migrator, to coastal Texas, Mexico and Central America
Food:	insects
Compare:	Yellow Warbler (p. 363) is brighter yellow with orange streaking on the male's chest. Male American Goldfinch (p. 357) has a black forehead and black wings. The male Common Yellowthroat (p. 359) has a very distinctive black mask.

Stan's Notes: A widespread warbler seen during migration and in winter. Can be found near water in willow and alder thickets. Its all-insect diet makes it one of the top insect-eating birds in North America. Often flicks its tail and spreads its wings when hopping among thick shrubs, looking for insects. Females often mate with males that have the best territories and that might already have mates (polygyny).

male

female

Lesser Goldfinch
Spinus psaltria

Size: 4½" (11 cm)

Male: Striking bright yellow beneath from chin to base of tail. Black head, tail and wings. White patches on wings. Eastern variety has a black back. Western has a green back.

Female: dull yellow underneath, lacks a black head and back

Juvenile: same as female

Nest: cup; female builds; 1–2 broods per year

Eggs: 4–5; pale blue without markings

Incubation: 10–12 days; female incubates

Fledging: 12–14 days; female and male feed young

Migration: partial migrator to non-migrator; will move around the state to find food

Food: seeds, insects; will come to seed feeders

Compare: The male American Goldfinch (p. 357) is slightly larger and has a yellow back, unlike the greenish back of male eastern Lesser Goldfinch or the black back of male western Lesser Goldfinch. The female American Goldfinch (p. 357) is larger and has darker wings than female Lesser Goldfinch.

Stan's Notes: There are two varieties of Lesser Goldfinch. Eastern males are found in eastern and southern Texas. Western males are found in Arizona. Prefers forest edges with a consistent water source. Unlike many other birds, its diet is about 96 percent seed, even during peak insect season. Will come to seed feeders. Late summer nesters. Male feeds the incubating female by regurgitating seeds. Pairs stay together all winter. Winter flocks can number in the hundreds.

American Goldfinch
Spinus tristis

WINTER

Size: 5" (13 cm)

Male: Canary-yellow finch with a black forehead and tail. Black wings with white wing bars. White rump. No markings on the chest. Winter male is similar to the female.

Female: dull olive-yellow plumage with brown wings; lacks a black forehead

Juvenile: same as female

Nest: cup; female builds; 1 brood per year

Eggs: 4–6; pale blue without markings

Incubation: 10–12 days; female incubates

Fledging: 11–17 days; female and male feed the young

Migration: partial migrator to complete; small flocks of up to 20 birds move around to find food

Food: seeds, insects; will come to seed feeders

Compare: Male western and eastern Lesser Goldfinch (p. 355) have a greenish or black back, respectively. The Pine Siskin (p. 109) and female House Finch (p. 111) have streaked breasts. Male Yellow Warbler (p. 363) is all yellow with orange streaks on breast. Male Wilson's Warbler (p. 353) lacks black wings.

Stan's Notes: Most often found in open fields, scrubby areas and woodlands. Enjoys Nyjer seed in feeders. Lines its nest with the silky down from wild thistle. Almost always in small flocks. Twitters while it flies. Flight is roller coaster-like. Often called Wild Canary due to the male's canary-colored plumage. Male sings a pleasant, high-pitched song.

male

female

Common Yellowthroat
Geothlypis trichas

YEAR-ROUND
SUMMER
WINTER

Size: 5" (13 cm)

Male: Olive-brown with a bright-yellow throat and chest, a white belly and a distinctive black mask outlined in white. Long, thin, pointed black bill.

Female: similar to male but lacks a black mask

Juvenile: same as female

Nest: cup; female builds; 2 broods per year

Eggs: 3–5; white with brown markings

Incubation: 11–12 days; female incubates

Fledging: 10–11 days; female and male feed the young

Migration: complete, to Mexico and Central America; non-migrator in far southeastern Arizona

Food: insects

Compare: The male American Goldfinch (p. 357) has a black forehead and wings. Male Yellow Warbler (p. 363) has fine orange streaks on chest and lacks the black mask. The Yellow-rumped Warbler (p. 251) only has patches of yellow and lacks the yellow chest of the Yellowthroat. Male Wilson's Warbler (p. 353) lacks the Yellowthroat's black mask.

Stan's Notes: A common warbler of open fields and marshes. Sings a cheerful, well-known "witchity-witchity-witchity-witchity" song from deep within tall grasses. Male sings from prominent perches and while he hunts. He performs a curious courtship display, bouncing in and out of tall grass while singing a mating song. Female builds a nest low to the ground. Young remain dependent on their parents longer than most other warblers. A frequent cowbird host.

Orange-crowned Warbler
Oreothlypis celata

Size: 5" (13 cm)

Male: An overall pale-yellow bird with a dark line through eyes. Faint streaking on sides and chest. Tawny-orange crown, often invisible. Small thin bill.

Female: same as male, but very slightly duller, often indistinguishable in the field

Juvenile: same as adults

Nest: cup; female builds; 1–2 broods per year

Eggs: 3–6; white with brown markings

Incubation: 12–14 days; female incubates

Fledging: 8–10 days; female and male feed young

Migration: complete, to southern Arizona, California, Mexico and Central America

Food: insects, fruit, nectar

Compare: Lucy's Warbler (p. 231) is smaller and has a rusty orange rump and a more noticeable orange crown. Yellow Warbler (p. 363) is brighter yellow with orange streaking on the male's chest. Wilson's Warbler (p. 353) is also brighter yellow with a distinct black cap. Male Common Yellowthroat (p. 359) has a distinctive black mask.

Stan's Notes: This widespread warbler can be seen year-round in Arizona, but is frequently seen more during migration when large groups move together. Builds a bulky, well-concealed nest on the ground with nest rim at ground level. Known to drink flower nectar. The orange crown tends to be hidden and is rarely seen in the field. A widespread breeder, from western Texas to Alaska and across Canada.

Yellow Warbler
Setophaga petechia

SUMMER
MIGRATION
WINTER

Size: 5" (13 cm)

Male: Yellow with thin orange streaks on the chest and belly. Long, pointed dark bill.

Female: same as male but lacks orange streaks

Juvenile: similar to female but much duller

Nest: cup; female builds; 1 brood per year

Eggs: 4–5; white with brown markings

Incubation: 11–12 days; female incubates

Fledging: 10–12 days; female and male feed the young

Migration: complete, to parts of western Arizona, Mexico, and Central and South America

Food: insects

Compare: Look for orange streaking on chest of male. Orange-crowned Warbler (p. 361) is paler yellow. Male American Goldfinch (p. 357) has black wings and forehead. The female Yellow Warbler is similar to the female American Goldfinch (p. 357), but it lacks white wing bars. Similar to male Wilson's Warbler (p. 353), which has a black cap, and lacks streaks on chest and belly.

Stan's Notes: Most widespread and second-most common warbler in the state, seen in gardens and shrubby areas near water. A prolific insect eater, gleaning caterpillars and other insects from tree leaves. Male sings a string of notes that sound like "sweet, sweet, sweet, I'm-so-sweet!" Begins to migrate south in August. Returns in late April. Males arrive in spring before females to claim territories. Migrates at night in mixed flocks of warblers. Rests and feeds during the day.

male

non-breeding male

female

Western Tanager
Piranga ludoviciana

Size: 7¼" (18.5 cm)

Male: A canary-yellow bird with a red head. Black back, tail, wings. One white and one yellow wing bar. Non-breeding lacks the red head.

Female: duller than male, lacking the red head

Juvenile: similar to female

Nest: cup; female builds; 1 brood per year

Eggs: 3–5; light blue with brown markings

Incubation: 14–18 days; female incubates

Fledging: 16–20 days; female and male feed young

Migration: complete, to Mexico and Central America

Food: insects, fruit

Compare: Male American Goldfinch (p. 357) has a black forehead and lacks breeding Western male's red head. Female Summer Tanager (p. 341) lacks wing bars. Female Bullock's and Scott's Orioles (pp. 333 and 373) lack female Western's single yellow wing bars.

Stan's Notes: Common throughout most of Arizona. The male is stunning in its breeding plumage. Feeds mainly on insects, such as bees, wasps, cicadas and grasshoppers, and to a lesser degree on fruit. The male feeds the female while she incubates. Female builds a cup nest in a horizontal fork of a coniferous tree, well away from the main trunk, 20–40 feet (6–12 m) aboveground. This is the farthest-nesting tanager species, reaching far up into the Northwest Territories of Canada. An early fall migrant, often seen migrating in late July (when non-breeding males lack red heads). Seen in many habitats during migration.

female

male
p. 341

Summer Tanager
Piranga rubra

SUMMER
MIGRATION

Size: 8" (20 cm)

Female: Some show a faint wash of red, but most females are a mustard-yellow overall with slightly darker wings.

Male: bright rosy-red bird with darker red wings

Juvenile: male has patches of red and green over the entire body, female is same as adult female

Nest: cup; female builds; 1–2 broods per year

Eggs: 3–5; pale blue with dark markings

Incubation: 10–12 days; female incubates

Fledging: 12–15 days; female and male feed young

Migration: complete, to Central and South America

Food: insects, fruit

Compare: Slightly larger than female Western Tanager (p. 365) and lacks the white and yellow wing bars. Female Scott's Oriole (p. 373) and Bullock's Oriole (p. 369) have white wing bars and lack the Summer Tanager's thicker bill.

Stan's Notes: Found in Arizona where woodlands exist, especially in mixed pine and oak forests. Due to clearing of land for agriculture, populations have decreased for over a century and especially most recently. Returning to the state in late April and with young hatching in late May, some pairs have two broods per year. While fruit makes up some of the diet, most of it consists of insects such as bees and wasps. Summer Tanagers unfortunately seem to be parasitized by Brown-headed and Bronzed Cowbirds.

male
p. 333

female

Bullock's Oriole
Icterus bullockii

Size: 8" (20 cm)

Female: Dull-yellow head and chest. Gray-to-black wings with white wing bars. A pale-white belly. Gray back, as seen in flight.

Male: bright-orange-and-black bird with a bold white patch on wings

Juvenile: similar to female

Nest: pendulous; female and male build; 1 brood per year

Eggs: 4–6; pale white to gray, brown markings

Incubation: 12–14 days; female incubates

Fledging: 12–14 days; female and male feed young

Migration: complete, to Mexico and Central America

Food: insects, berries, nectar; visits nectar feeders

Compare: Female Scott's Oriole (p. 373) is larger and lacks the pale-white belly. Female Western Tanager (p. 365) has a black back unlike the female Oriole's gray back. Female Summer Tanager (p. 367) lacks wing bars. Look for the overall dull-yellow and gray appearance of the female Bullock's Oriole.

Stan's Notes: So closely related to Baltimore Orioles of the eastern U.S., at one time both were considered a single species. Interbreeds with Baltimores where their ranges overlap. Most common in the state where cottonwood trees grow alongside rivers and other wetlands. Also found at edges of clearings, in city parks, on farms and along irrigation ditches. Hanging sock-like nest is constructed of plant fibers such as inner bark of junipers and willows.

male

female

juvenile

Evening Grosbeak
Coccothraustes vespertinus

Size: 8" (20 cm)

Male: Striking bird with bright-yellow eyebrows, rump and belly. Black-and-white wings and tail. Dark, dirty-yellow head and large, thick ivory-to-greenish bill.

Female: similar to male, with softer colors and a gray head and throat

Juvenile: similar to female, with a brown bill

Nest: cup; female builds; 1 brood per year

Eggs: 3–4; blue with brown markings

Incubation: 12–14 days; female incubates

Fledging: 13–14 days; female and male feed young

Migration: irruptive; moves around the state in search of food

Food: seeds, insects, fruit; comes to seed feeders

Compare: The American Goldfinch (p. 357) is closely related, but it is much smaller. Look for the yellow eyebrows and thick bill to identify the Evening Grosbeak.

Stan's Notes: One of the largest finches. Characteristic finch-like undulating flight. Uses its unusually large bill to crack seeds, its main food source. Often seen on gravel roads eating gravel, which provides minerals, salt and grit to grind the seeds it eats. A year-round resident in eastern Arizona, it is more obvious during the winter because it moves in large flocks, searching for food, often coming to feeders. Sheds the outer layer of its bill during spring, exposing a blue-green bill.

male

female

Scott's Oriole
Icterus parisorum

SUMMER

Size: 9" (22.5 cm)

Male: Black head, neck, back, upper breast and tail. Lemon-yellow belly, shoulders and rump. Long, pointed, slightly down-curved black bill. Dark eyes. Two white wing bars.

Female: similar to male, but has much less black

Juvenile: grayer than female, yellow under belly only

Nest: pendulous; female builds; 1–2 broods a year

Eggs: 2–4; pale blue with brown markings

Incubation: 14–16 days; female and male incubate

Fledging: 14–16 days; female and male feed young

Migration: complete, to Mexico

Food: insects, fruit, nectar; will come to orange or grapefruit halves and nectar feeders

Compare: The female Bullock's Oriole (p. 369) has a pale-white belly. Male American Goldfinch (p. 357) is much smaller and has black on the forehead, not on the entire head.

Stan's Notes: Found in open dry areas often associated with yucca and palm. Like other oriole species, female constructs a sock like pouch that hangs from the end of a thin branch or is woven into a hole in a palm leaf. Populations have increased over the past 100 years due to planting of palm trees. Male is yellow, not orange, like other male orioles. Hunts by gleaning insects and caterpillars from leaves. Uses its long pointed bill to poke holes in bases of flowers to get nectar. Parents feed their young by regurgitating a mixture of insects and fruit. Named after General Winfield Scott, who fought in the Mexican War.

Western Kingbird
Tyrannus verticalis

Size: 9" (22.5 cm)

Male: Bright-yellow belly and yellow under wings. Gray head and chest, often with white chin. Wings and tail are dark gray to nearly black with white outer edges on tail.

Female: same as male

Juvenile: similar to adult, less yellow and more gray

Nest: cup; female and male construct; 1 brood per year

Eggs: 3–4; white with brown markings

Incubation: 18–20 days; female incubates

Fledging: 16–18 days; female and male feed young

Migration: complete, to Central America

Food: insects, berries

Compare: Western Meadowlark (p. 377) shares the yellow belly of Western Kingbird, but it has a distinctive black V-shaped necklace.

Stan's Notes: A bird of open country, frequently seen sitting on top of the same shrub or fence post. Hunts by watching for crickets, bees, grasshoppers and other insects and flying out to catch them, then returns to perch. Parents teach young how to hunt, bringing wounded insects back to the nest for the young to chase. Returns in March. Builds nest in April, often in a fork of a small single-trunk tree. Common throughout the state, where nearly every stand of trees around a homestead or farm is home to a pair of Western Kingbirds. Some may winter in southeastern Arizona.

Western Meadowlark

Sturnella neglecta

YEAR-ROUND
WINTER

Size: 9" (22.5 cm)

Male: Heavy-bodied bird with a short tail. Yellow chest and brown back. Prominent V-shaped black necklace. White outer tail feathers.

Female: same as male

Juvenile: same as adult

Nest: cup, on the ground in dense cover; female builds; 2 broods per year

Eggs: 3–5; white with brown markings

Incubation: 13–15 days; female incubates

Fledging: 11–13 days; female and male feed young

Migration: non-migrator to partial migrator; moves around in winter to find food

Food: insects, seeds

Compare: Western Kingbird (p. 375) shares the yellow belly, but it lacks the V-shaped black necklace. Look for a black V marking on the chest to help identify the Meadowlark.

Stan's Notes: Most common in open country. Named "Meadowlark" because it's a bird of meadows and sings like the larks of Europe. Not in the lark family; it's a member of the blackbird family. Best known for its wonderful song—a flute-like, clear whistle. Often seen perching on fence posts but quickly dives into tall grass when approached. Like other members of the blackbird family, the meadowlark catches prey by poking its long thin bill in places such as holes in the ground or tufts of grass, where insects are hiding. Conspicuous white marks on sides of tail, seen when flying away.

BIRDING ON THE INTERNET

Birding online is a great way to discover additional information and learn more about birds. These websites will assist
you in your pursuit of birds. Web addresses sometimes
change a bit, so if one no longer works, just enter the name of
the group into a search engine to track down the new address.

Site	Address
Author Stan Tekiela's homepage	naturesmart.com
American Birding Association	aba.org
Arizona Raptor Center	arizonaraptorcenter.org
Arizona's Raptor Experience	arizonasraptorexperience.com
Audubon Arizona	az.audubon.org
The Cornell Lab of Ornithology	birds.cornell.edu
eBird	ebird.org
International Raptor & Falconry Center	raptorfalconrycenter.org
Maricopa Audubon Society	www.maricopaaudubon.org
Northern Arizona Audubon Society	www.northernarizonaaudubon.org
Rio Salado Audubon Center	riosalado.audubon.org
Tucson Audubon Society	tucsonaudubon.org

CHECKLIST/INDEX BY SPECIES

Use the boxes to check the birds you've seen.

MORE FOR ARIZONA BY STAN TEKIELA

Identification Guides

Birds of Prey of the West
Field Guide

Cactus of Arizona Field Guide

Mammals of Arizona Field Guide

Trees of Arizona Field Guide

Wildflowers of Arizona
Field Guide

Children's Books: Adventure Board Book Series

Floppers & Loppers

Paws & Claws

Peepers & Peekers

Snouts & Sniffers

Children's Books

C is for Cardinal

Can You Count the Critters?

Critter Litter

Critter Litter Southwest

Children's Books: Wildlife Picture Books

Baby Bear Discovers the World

The Cutest Critter

Do Beavers Need Blankets?

Hidden Critters

Jump, Little Wood Ducks

Some Babies Are Wild

Super Animal Powers

What Eats That?

Whose Baby Butt?

Whose Butt?

Whose House Is That?

Whose Track Is That?

Adventure Quick Guides

Birds of the Southwest

ABOUT THE AUTHOR

Naturalist, wildlife photographer and writer Stan Tekiela is the originator of the popular state-specific field guide series that includes the *Trees of Arizona Field Guide*. Stan has authored more than 190 educational books, including field guides, quick guides, nature books, children's books, and more, presenting many species of animals and plants.

With a Bachelor of Science degree in natural history from the University of Minnesota and as an active professional naturalist for more than 30 years, Stan studies and photographs wildlife throughout the United States and Canada. He has received national and regional awards for his books and photographs and is also a well-known columnist and radio personality. His syndicated column appears in more than 25 newspapers, and his wildlife programs are broadcast on a number of Midwest radio stations. You can follow Stan on Facebook and Twitter or contact him via his website, naturesmart.com.